Comfort Zone

A 40-day Devotional on the Father of All Comfort

NOLA LORRAINE

Comfort Zone: A 40-day Devotional on the Father of All Comfort
© Nola Lorraine 2025

Published by Armour Books
P. O. Box 492, Corinda QLD 4075 AUSTRALIA

Cover image: Forgiven Photography | Lightstock;
Author photo by Wayne Logan at Encouraging Photos

Illustrations, icons & section divider images: Beckon Creative;
wings by DesignScotch | Creative Fabrica;
feathers by Elena Dorosh | Creative Market

Interior design and typeset by Beckon Creative

ISBN 978-1-925380-85-9

 A catalogue record for this book is available from the National Library of Australia

All Rights Reserved. No part of this work may be reproduced, stored in, or introduced into a retrieval system, or transmitted, in any form, or by any means (electronic, mechanical, photocopying, recording or otherwise) without the prior written permission of the publisher.

Scripture quotations marked AMP are taken from the Amplified Version of the Bible Copyright © 2015 by The Lockman Foundation, La Habra, CA 90631. All rights reserved. www.lockman.org

Scripture quotations marked ESV are taken from the ESV® Bible (The Holy Bible, English Standard Version®), copyright © 2001 by Crossway, a publishing ministry of Good News Publishers. Used by permission. All rights reserved.

Scripture quotations marked GNT are from the Good News Translation in Today's English Version—Second Edition Copyright © 1992 by American Bible Society. Used by Permission.

Scripture quotations marked NAS are taken from the New American Standard Bible®, Copyright © 1960, 1962, 1963, 1968, 1971, 1972, 1973, 1975, 1977, 1995 by The Lockman Foundation. Used by permission. www.lockman.org

Scripture quotations marked NIV are taken from the Holy Bible, New International Version®, NIV®. Copyright © 1973, 1978, 1984, 2011 by Biblica, Inc.™ Used by permission of Zondervan. All rights reserved worldwide. www.zondervan.com The "NIV" and "New International Version" are trademarks registered in the United States Patent and Trademark Office by Biblica, Inc.™.

Scripture quotations marked NLT are taken from the Holy Bible, New Living Translation, copyright 1996, 2004. Used by permission of Tyndale House Publishers, Inc., Wheaton, Illinois 60189. All rights reserved.

All quoted Bible verses have been taken from the versions that appear on Bible Hub.

*Comfort,
comfort My people...*

Isaiah 40:1 NIV

Dedication

For my husband and soulmate, Tim.

You have been my biggest source of support
and encouragement since the day we met.
We've laughed with each other in the good times
and comforted each other in the
challenging times.
I am so blessed that God brought us together
and that we can partner with Him
for the Kingdom.
Thank you for helping me to reach for my dreams.
I love you more than words can say.

Contents

Introduction		9
Day 1	The Father of All Comfort	12
Day 2	God's Rescue Mission	16
Day 3	A Father Like No Other	20
Day 4	Adopted as God's Children	24
Day 5	The Family of God	28
Day 6	The Ministry of Hospitality	32
Day 7	A Surpassing Love	36
Day 8	Can a Mother Forget?	40
Day 9	A Father Who Delights	44
Day 10	The God Who Sees Me	48
Day 11	The God Who Hears Me	52
Day 12	A Touch from the Lord	56
Day 13	Tasting the Goodness of God	60
Day 14	An Aroma Pleasing to God	64
Day 15	The Fragrance of Gifts	68
Day 16	The God Who Acts	72
Day 17	God Cares for Your Needs	76

Day 18	Helping Others Now	80
Day 19	Jesus the Good Shepherd	84
Day 20	A God Who Sympathises	88
Day 21	Tears in a Bottle	92
Day 22	The Holy Spirit, Our Comforter	96
Day 23	A God Who Intercedes	100
Day 24	Be an Advocate	104
Day 25	God, Our Creator	108
Day 26	Made in His Image	112
Day 27	Love Others	116
Day 28	A Good Neighbour	120
Day 29	The Least of These	124
Day 30	A God of Refuge	128
Day 31	Walking on the Heights	132
Day 32	His Grace is Sufficient	136
Day 33	When it's Not Your Fault	140
Day 34	When the Fault Lies with You	144
Day 35	He Works for Our Good	150
Day 36	Rememering Past Victories	154
Day 37	Ripples of Kindness	158
Day 38	Never Forsaken	164
Day 39	Feed My Sheep	168
Day 40	Joy in the Morning	172
Acknowledgements		177

Introduction

The world needs a collective hug.

Wars, natural disasters and a pandemic have taken their toll on millions. At a personal level, people also struggle with relationship issues, employment, finances, health, bereavement and a myriad of other concerns that vie for attention. Where is God in all of this?

I struggled with that question when I found myself going through a desert time. If God cares about me, He would have answered that particular prayer or worked things out in the way I expected. It's taken my heart a while to catch up with what I already knew in my head. God was right there. He hadn't left me, but I was keeping Him at arm's length.

Have you ever tried to give someone a hug, only to have them stiffen or awkwardly move aside?

I've been that person at times, knowing God's comfort was there yet not fully embracing it. But God is gentle, always ready to reach out to us with a tender word and a healing touch.

In his second letter to the Corinthians, Paul reminds the believers of their true source of comfort:

Praise be to the God and Father of our Lord Jesus Christ, the Father of compassion and the God of all comfort, who comforts us in all our troubles, so that we can comfort those in any trouble with the comfort we ourselves receive from God.

2 Corinthians 1:3–4 NIV

As I let that scripture seep into my soul, I realised I hadn't always sought God's comfort first. He might be sixth on the list after whinging to my husband, cuddling the dog, going for a walk, watching funny film clips or eating a jumbo bag of chips in one sitting.

If you've ever found yourself in that sort of situation, take heart. God's love, comfort, grace, encouragement and support are limitless. If we reach out and allow Him to do His work in us, we will experience His comfort and His strength in ever-increasing measure. Not only that, but we can then take the comfort we have received from God and pass it on to others.

I'm still on my journey, and you'll read about some

of my experiences in these devotions. However, I want to put these verses into action and share with you some of what I've learned. You'll find reflections on the nature of God's love and comfort and how we can receive that love and comfort for ourselves. However, God also wants us to get out of our *Comfort Zone* and pass on that love and comfort to others. I've included some devotions on that topic in this book, but stay tuned for the second book in this series—*No Standing Zone*. In that volume, I'll delve more into how we can keep moving forward with God in terms of both our own spiritual journeys and the tasks He has for us to do in partnership with Him.

As you work through these devotions, may you gain a deeper understanding of what it means to be a precious child of God. May the Father of all Comfort speak to you through His Word and give you the peace, joy and strength He longs for you to have.

Your fellow traveller

Nola

Comfort Zone

Day 1

Key Verse

Praise be to the God and Father of our Lord Jesus Christ, the Father of compassion and the God of all comfort, who comforts us in all our troubles, so that we can comfort those in any trouble with the comfort we ourselves receive from God.

2 Corinthians 1:3–4 NIV

Reading

Praise be to the God and Father of our Lord Jesus Christ, the Father of compassion and the God of all comfort, who comforts us in all our troubles, so that we can comfort those in any trouble with the comfort we ourselves receive from God. For just as we share abundantly in the sufferings of Christ, so also our comfort abounds through Christ. If we are distressed, it is for your comfort and salvation; if we are comforted, it is for your comfort, which produces in you patient endurance of the same sufferings we suffer. And our hope for you is firm, because we know that just as you share in our sufferings, so also you share in our comfort.

2 Corinthians 1:3–7 NIV

The Father of All Comfort

Reflect

I grew up knowing that I was adopted as a baby, but I didn't really start working through the issue until my thirties. I was doing a counselling course with a missionary organisation, and we had to answer the question *'Who Am I?'* as one of our homework exercises. God put His finger on my heart at that moment and told me it was time to work through my issues of identity and abandonment, among other things.

It was a challenging time, but I really appreciated the support and encouragement of the counselling staff and fellow students. When we later went on a counselling outreach to New Zealand, I was able to get up in front of a room full of people and share a testimony of how God was helping me with those issues. I still had a lot of work to do, but it was good to be able to pass on some of the comfort and hope God had given me.

We can find comfort from many sources. Some may be helpful (e.g., caring friends and family members), while others may be harmful (e.g., addictive behaviours). However, God is our true source of comfort. The Greek word for comfort is *paraklesis*, which has the same root as that used to describe the Holy Spirit in John 14:16. The image is of one coming alongside us in our struggles and offering support and encouragement. But it doesn't stop there. God wants us to take the comfort we've received from Him and pass it on to others who are struggling. Let's partner with Him to heal a hurting world.

Pray

Dear Lord, thank you for the countless times you've comforted me in my times of need. Please show me how I can pass on Your encouragement and support to others. *Amen*.

Apply

① Read 2 Corinthians 7:5–7. Paul had written a letter to the Corinthians, highlighting some issues they needed to address. How was God's comfort passed on in this situation?

② How could you comfort others with the comfort you have received from God?

Day 1

God is our true source of comfort.

Comfort Zone

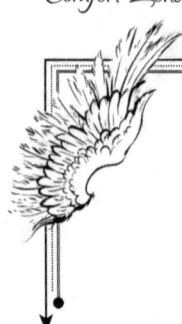

Day 2

Key Verse

For God so loved the world that He gave His one and only Son, that whoever believes in Him shall not perish but have eternal life. For God did not send His Son into the world to condemn the world, but to save the world through Him.

John 3:16–17 NIV

Reading

Once you were dead because of your disobedience and your many sins. You used to live in sin, just like the rest of the world, obeying the devil—the commander of the powers in the unseen world. He is the spirit at work in the hearts of those who refuse to obey God. All of us used to live that way, following the passionate desires and inclinations of our sinful nature. By our very nature we were subject to God's anger, just like everyone else. But God is so rich in mercy, and He loved us so much, that even though we were dead because of our sins, He gave us life when He raised Christ from the dead. (It is only by God's grace that you have been saved!) For He raised us from the

Day 2

God's Rescue Mission

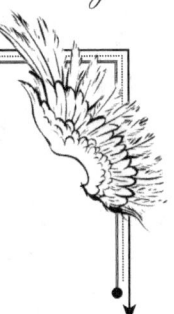

dead along with Christ and seated us with Him in the heavenly realms because we are united with Christ Jesus. So God can point to us in all future ages as examples of the incredible wealth of His grace and kindness toward us, as shown in all He has done for us who are united with Christ Jesus. God saved you by His grace when you believed. And you can't take credit for this; it is a gift from God. Salvation is not a reward for the good things we have done, so none of us can boast about it. For we are God's masterpiece. He has created us anew in Christ Jesus, so we can do the good things He planned for us long ago.

Ephesians 2:1–10 NLT

Reflect

After our two beautiful dogs died in the same year, my husband and I decided to buy an older dog from a shelter rather than looking for another puppy. We adopted Penny, a lovely five-year-old corgi mix, who needed a new home after her elderly owner passed away. A few months later, I found out that her previous owner's daughter had initially rung the shelter to ask for advice. She wasn't in a position to look after Penny herself and she wondered if it would be kinder to have her put down rather than risk her going to a bad family. Fortunately, the shelter employee assured the woman that they would find her a good home. Penny was literally rescued from death.

If God cared enough to save that little dog, how much more does He care for us? We were destined for death because of our sin, but God saved us by sending His beloved Son Jesus to die in our place. Indeed, Jesus' mission on earth was 'to seek and to save the lost' (Luke 19:10 NIV). Through Him, we have forgiveness of sin. Our debt has been wiped clean. There was nothing we could do to save ourselves. It was an act of God's compassion and grace to us. It is a free gift, with no strings attached. Like any gift, however, we can choose to accept it or reject it. Our choice has eternal consequences. What will you do with His precious gift?

Day 2

Pray

Dear Lord, thank You for Your priceless gift in sending Your only Son to die for our sins. Thank You that through Him, we have eternal life. Please help me to live a life of gratitude for all You have done for me. *Amen*.

Apply

① Read Ephesians 2:1–10 again. What stands out to you most about what God has done for us?

② Have you accepted God's free gift of salvation? If so, thank Him for all He has done for you. If you haven't yet accepted God's gift of salvation, is there anything that would stop you from asking Him to come into your heart right now?

Day 3

Key Verse

See what great love the Father has lavished on us, that we should be called children of God!

1 John 3:1a NIV

Reading

Dear friends, let us love one another, for love comes from God. Everyone who loves has been born of God and knows God. Whoever does not love does not know God, because God is love. This is how God showed His love among us: He sent His one and only Son into the world that we might live through Him. This is love: not that we loved God, but that He loved us and sent His Son as an atoning sacrifice for our sins. Dear friends, since God so loved us, we also ought to love one another. No one has ever seen God; but if we love one another, God lives in us and His love is made complete in us.

1 John 4:7–12 NIV

A Father Like No Other

Reflect

My dad lived in a nursing home with Mum for more than five years, and recently passed away at the age of ninety-two. He was a loving father and I'm glad I had him in my life for so long. I have many happy memories, including our last Father's Day together. However, Father's Day can bring about a mix of emotions. I never knew my birthfather and have no way of even knowing who he is. My husband and I were unable to have children, so Father's Day is not something we celebrate as a family. I've known many people who've had wonderful fathers, but I've known others who have absent fathers, are estranged from their fathers or have been abused by their fathers.

Regardless of the experience we've had with our earthly fathers, there is one thing we can be sure of. God is the good and perfect Father who always has our best interests at heart. His care for us is limitless. His love is all-consuming. He hasn't just given us a bit of His love. He's lavished His love on us. He not only embodies love or reflects love. He IS love.

Until we really understand the magnitude of what He's done for us in sending Jesus to die for us, we'll never understand His love or His comfort. We can only love others, because He first loved us. As we meditate on today's reading, may the Word sink deep into our hearts. We are the children of a Father who loves us like no other.

Pray

Dear Lord, it's hard for us to grasp the magnitude of what You've done for us in sending Jesus to die for our sins. Thank You that You first loved us and that we are Your children. Help us to receive Your love so that we can pass it on to a world in need of You. *Amen*.

Apply

① Do you find it easy or difficult to accept God's love? Why or why not?

② Read over 1 John 4:7–12 several times, noting what it says about the love of God. Spend time meditating on it and thanking God for His boundless love.

Day 3

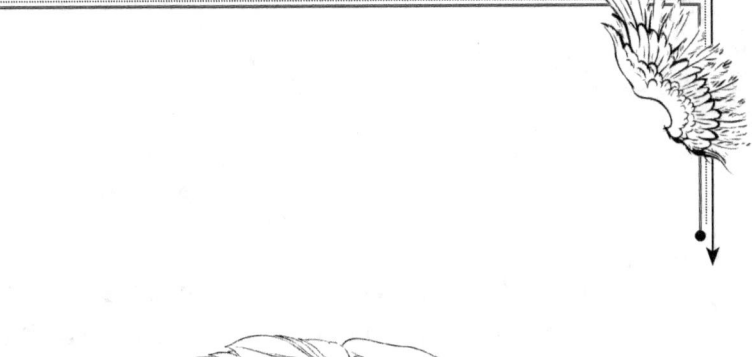

"God is the good and perfect Father who always has our best interests at heart."

Comfort Zone

Day 4

Key Verse

For you did not receive the spirit of slavery to fall back into fear, but you have received the Spirit of adoption as sons, by whom we cry, 'Abba! Father!'

Romans 8:15 ESV

Reading

For all who are led by the Spirit of God are sons of God. For you did not receive the spirit of slavery to fall back into fear, but you have received the Spirit of adoption as sons, by whom we cry, 'Abba! Father!' The Spirit Himself bears witness with our spirit that we are children of God, and if children, then heirs— heirs of God and fellow-heirs with Christ, provided we suffer with Him in order that we may also be glorified with Him.

Romans 8:14–17 ESV

Day 4

Adopted as God's Children

Reflect

In our society, adoption can conjure up different images in people's minds. Some may see it as a good and charitable thing to do. If a child's biological parents can't raise the child themselves, for whatever reason, then it's a kind gesture to adopt the child and give them the best chance at life. However, it can also come with more negative connotations. If a couple can't have their own children, then they might be able to adopt a child, though that's not always easy these days. The implication is that adoption is Plan B, not the more desired Plan A.

However, adoption wasn't second-best in Biblical times. F.F. Bruce notes that 'an adopted son was a son deliberately chosen by his adoptive father to perpetuate his name and inherit his estate; he was [not] inferior in status to a son born in the ordinary course of nature, and might well enjoy the father's affection more fully and reproduce the father's character more worthily.'[1]

---

1 Bruce, F.F. (1963). *The epistle of Paul to the Romans: An introduction and commentary.* Leicester: InterVarity Press.

God has deliberately chosen us to be adopted as His children. We have full rights as His heirs. We are not second-best. The Aramaic word 'Abba' is only used three times in the New Testament—once by Jesus in the Garden of Gethsemane (Mark 14:36) and again in two references to adoption as God's sons (Romans 8:15; Galatians 4:6). It is a more affectionate and informal way of addressing a natural father, much as we might say 'Daddy' or 'Papa' today. It's mind-blowing to think that the God of the universe is also our Abba, Father. Let's thank Him for His incredible gift.

Pray

Dear Lord, thank You that You have adopted me as Your child and that, like Jesus, I can cry out 'Abba, Father' to You. Help me to grasp more fully what it means to be Your child. *Amen.*

Day 4

Apply

① Read Romans 8:13–17 and Galatians 3:26–4:7. What are the differences between a slave and a son (or child) of God?

② What does it mean to you personally to know that you have been adopted as a child of God?

An adopted child was a child deliberately chosen.

Comfort Zone

Day 5

Key Verse

God places the lonely in families.

Psalm 68:6a NLT

Reading

All the believers devoted themselves to the apostles' teaching, and to fellowship, and to sharing in meals (including the Lord's Supper), and to prayer. A deep sense of awe came over them all, and the apostles performed many miraculous signs and wonders. And all the believers met together in one place and shared everything they had. They sold their property and possessions and shared the money with those in need. They worshipped together at the Temple each day, met in homes for the Lord's Supper, and shared their meals with great joy and generosity—all the while praising God and enjoying the goodwill of all the people. And each day the Lord added to their fellowship those who were being saved.

Acts 2:42–47 NLT

Day 5

The Family of God

Reflect

I grew up as an only child and always missed having siblings. I especially wanted a sister and I remember asking my mum for one when I was about six years old. I thought it would be fun to have someone at home to play with whenever I wanted. I had friends at school and Sunday school, but that wasn't the same as having someone 'on tap' at home. In my thirties, my main motivation for searching for my birthmother was that I wondered if I had siblings. Sadly, she had passed away before I started looking for her and it appears she had no other children. Now in my sixties, I still miss having that close connection to a sibling.

However, God has been faithful in providing me with many close friends throughout my life, starting with my first friend as a three-year-old in Sunday School. I may not have a biological sister, but God has given me many sisters in the faith who have been as close as a sibling to me. That's the great thing about God's family. It's not dependent on biological ties, but on spiritual connections. We all have the same Heavenly Father and we are a community of believers.

The early church, described in Acts, is a good model of what that family should look like. They ate together, worshipped together, learned about God together, fellowshipped with one another and shared what they had with whoever was in need. Their love for one another was a witness to those outside the faith and God swelled their ranks daily with those who were being saved. No matter what kind of earthly family we have or don't have, let's always remember that we are part of God's family of believers.

Pray

Dear Lord, thank You that if we have put our trust in You, we are part of Your family of believers. Thank You for the many spiritual sisters, brothers, mothers and fathers You have given us; and help us to reflect Your love in return. *Amen*.

Day 5

Apply

① Read Acts 2:42–47 and 4:32–35. What were the main characteristics of the family of believers in the early church?

② Do you belong to a local fellowship or an online community of believers? If not, seek out possible opportunities in your area and try connecting with one today.

> *We are part of God's family of believers.*

Day 6

Key Verse

Share with the Lord's people who are in need. Practice hospitality.

Romans 12:13 NIV

Reading

Dear friend [Gaius], you are faithful in what you are doing for the brothers and sisters, even though they are strangers to you. They have told the church about your love. Please send them on their way in a manner that honours God. It was for the sake of the Name that they went out, receiving no help from the pagans. We ought therefore to show hospitality to such people so that we may work together for the truth.

I wrote to the church, but Diotrephes, who loves to be first, will not welcome us. So when I come, I will call attention to what he is doing, spreading malicious nonsense about us. Not satisfied with that, he even refuses to welcome other believers. He also stops those who want to do so and puts them out of the church.

The Ministry of Hospitality

Dear friend, do not imitate what is evil but what is good. Anyone who does what is good is from God. Anyone who does what is evil has not seen God.

3 John 5–11 NIV

Reflect

I once went to Southern India on a short-term mission trip. After learning a few phrases in the local language, we set off in pairs to practise those words with people we met. My teammate and I soon came across a man sitting outside his house, so we tried to start a conversation. The few phrases I knew roughly translated as, 'Hello, my name is Nola and this is John. We are trying to learn your language. We cannot speak your language properly.'

The man spoke English and invited us into his home. His family prepared some food and drink for us, and he spent about an hour teaching us different words. We were overwhelmed with the hospitality the family showed us, especially as we were strangers from a different country and religion.

Hospitality is sometimes undervalued in western culture. I remember a young woman telling me that she had no trouble raising funds to go on a mission trip to Africa. But when she was asked to join the hospitality department of a missionary organisation, people weren't as interested in supporting her. Presumably, going on an outreach was seen as more important than showing hospitality to missionaries and taking care of their needs, but the apostle John didn't make such a distinction.

John commends Gaius for the love he'd shown to travelling missionaries. By doing so, he had partnered in their work. However, Diotrephes was more interested in his position. Not only did he fail to welcome other believers, but he tried to prevent others from doing so, even expelling them from his church. Thus, he was actually hindering the spread of the gospel.

There are many types of service, but hospitality is one way we can bless others and show them God's love. Will we be a Gaius or a Diotrephes?

Day 6

Pray

Dear Lord, thank You for the many times I've been the recipient of hospitality. Help me to share the love You have given me, by showing hospitality to others. *Amen.*

Apply

① Read Hebrews 13:1–2 and 1 Peter 4:9. What do those verses say about hospitality?

② Pray and ask God if there is someone you could extend hospitality to in the next couple of weeks.

Hospitality is one way we can bless others and show them God's love.

Day 7

Key Verse

And may you have the power to understand, as all God's people should, how wide, how long, how high, and how deep His love is.

Ephesians 3:18 NLT

Reading

When I think of all this, I fall to my knees and pray to the Father, the Creator of everything in heaven and on earth. I pray that from His glorious, unlimited resources He will empower you with inner strength through His Spirit. Then Christ will make His home in your hearts as you trust in Him. Your roots will grow down into God's love and keep you strong. And may you have the power to understand, as all God's people should, how wide, how long, how high, and how deep His love is. May you experience the love of Christ, though it is too great to understand fully. Then you will be made complete with all the fullness of life and power that comes from God.

Now all glory to God, who is able, through His mighty power at work within us, to accomplish infinitely

A Surpassing Love

more than we might ask or think. Glory to Him in the church and in Christ Jesus through all generations forever and ever! Amen.

Ephesians 3:14–21 NLT

Reflect

I was a late bloomer when it came to romantic relationships. I didn't have my first date until I was 18, and I only went on a handful of other dates over the years. I tried to stay hopeful, but it was easy to conclude that I must be unattractive or undesirable in some way. I finally had my first proper boyfriend at the age of 35, but I ended the relationship when some red flags shot up.

Then there was Tim. Early in our relationship, he presented me with a series of love letters that he'd been writing for me before we'd even gone on our first date. I was flabbergasted at the depth of emotion in them. He really loved me. *Me!* Well, it worked, because we've been married for 26 years and still going strong.

But as wonderful as Tim's love is, it pales in comparison to the love that Jesus has for us. The Apostle Paul prayed that the Ephesians would grasp something of that love, though it is beyond our complete comprehension. There's no end to it. It's wider, longer, higher and deeper than anything we can imagine. Yet as Christ dwells in our hearts, and we experience more and more of His presence in our lives, that love can sink further into our hearts and break any lies of the enemy that would make us feel unlovable. Let's draw on the strength of the One whose love never fades, and show Him our love in return.

Pray

Dear Lord, thank You that You love me with a depth I can't even imagine. Your love and care is beyond anything I could receive apart from You. Please always keep me grounded in Your love. *Amen*.

Day 7

Apply

① Read Lamentations 3:21–23. What does it mean to you to know that the love and compassion of the Lord never fails?

② Have you ever felt unloved or unlovable? Read Ephesians 3:14–21 slowly and personalise it as a prayer for yourself, asking God to show you how very much you are loved.

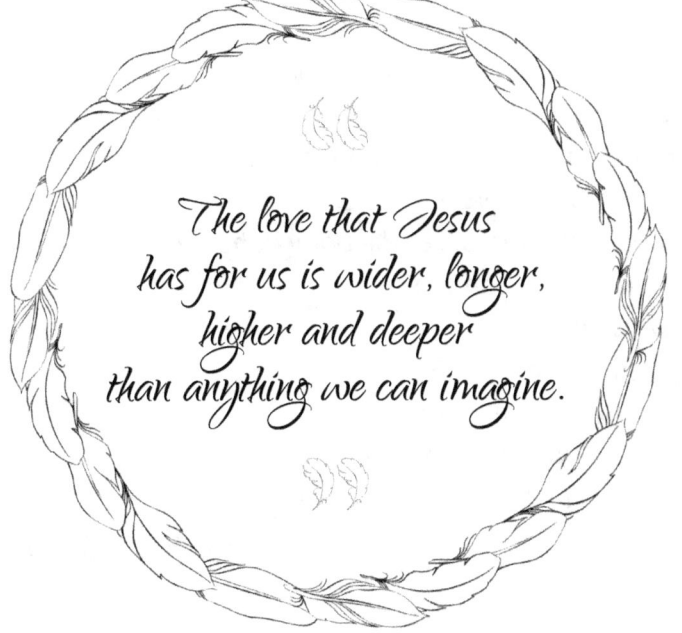

> The love that Jesus has for us is wider, longer, higher and deeper than anything we can imagine.

Comfort Zone

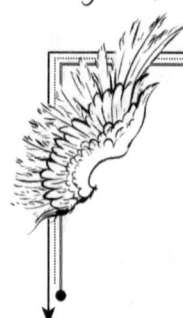

Day 8

Key Verse

See, I have engraved you on the palms of My hands.

Isaiah 49:16a NIV

Reading

Shout for joy, you heavens;
rejoice, you earth;
burst into song, you mountains!
For the Lord comforts His people
and will have compassion on His afflicted ones.
But Zion said, 'The Lord has forsaken me,
the Lord has forgotten me.'
'Can a mother forget the baby at her breast
and have no compassion on the child she
  has borne?
Though she may forget,
I will not forget you!
See, I have engraved you on the palms of My hands;
your walls are ever before Me.'

Isaiah 49:13–16 NIV

Can a Mother Forget?

Reflect

I was preschool age when my parents first told me I was adopted. I knew that meant they weren't my 'natural' parents, but it wasn't until my teenage years that I really started to consider how my adoption first required an abandonment. My biological mother had to give me up in order for my adoptive parents to take me up.

Sadly, my birthmother passed away about ten years before I started searching for her, so I was never able to find out her side of the story or learn the identity of my biological father. I know things were different in those days. Attitudes were less favourable towards unwed mothers and there weren't the supports that are in place today. She may have thought she was giving me the best chance possible by relinquishing me. I've had a good life with parents who loved me, but that doesn't completely take away the sadness of never knowing the parents who gave me life.

The people of Israel thought the Lord had forgotten them, but He replied: *'Can a mother forget the baby at her breast and have no compassion on the child she has borne? Though she may forget, I will not forget you! See, I have engraved you on the palms of My hands...'* (Isaiah 49:15–16a NIV).

I don't think my birthmother could have forgotten me. But God reminds us that even if our parents do forget us, He never does. It's as if He's inscribed our names with permanent ink that can never be washed away. Only He can heal us from those feelings of abandonment. He is indeed the loving Father who will never leave us.

Pray

Dear Lord, thank You that You are a loving Father who will never reject us, never abandon us, and never forget us. Thank You that my name is engraved on Your hands. Please help me to be the loving child You created me to be. *Amen.*

Apply

① Have you ever felt rejected or forgotten by a parent or someone else who was important to you? What comfort can you find in today's passage and Psalm 27:10?

② What does it mean for you to know that God has engraved you on the palms of His hands?

God will not forget you!

Comfort Zone

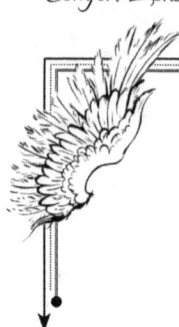

Day 9

Key Verse

The Lord your God is with you, the Mighty Warrior who saves. He will take great delight in you; in His love He will no longer rebuke you, but will rejoice over you with singing.

Zephaniah 3:17 NIV

Reading

Sing hymns of praise to the Lord;
play music on the harp to our God.
He spreads clouds over the sky;
He provides rain for the earth
and makes grass grow on the hills.
He gives animals their food
and feeds the young ravens when they call.
His pleasure is not in strong horses,
nor His delight in brave soldiers;
but He takes pleasure in those who honour Him,
in those who trust in His constant love.

Psalm 147:7–11 GNT

Day 9

A Father Who Delights

Reflect

I was sitting next to a young father and his daughter on a plane trip to Sydney. The little girl was about three years old and her dad had lots of things to keep her occupied—books, electronic devices, snacks and more.

However, these things were never used to distract the child or keep her busy so the father could get on with his own agenda. He was engaged with her the whole flight. He spoke to her in a kind and loving way. He used an animated voice when reading to her. He encouraged her during an educational game. He watched a short video with her. He took photos of her and explained things about the plane. He delighted in her and enjoyed spending time with her.

The girl also clearly loved being with her father. There was never the slightest hint of a tantrum. She smiled, she played, she answered Dad's questions and followed his instructions. Even when we were on the tarmac waiting to disembark, he was still connecting with her in a meaningful way.

As I watched this remarkable dad, I couldn't help thinking that's the kind of relationship God desires with us. He loves us and delights in us. It's not a burden for Him to interact with us. He wants to spend time with us, enjoy our company, show us the wonders of His world and give us instructions that bring life. This doesn't mean He delights in everything we do, as we will often make mistakes, but He loves and values us as His dear children. Let's take time to delight in the loving Father who delights in us.

Pray

Dear Lord, sometimes it's hard for me to imagine how You could delight in me. Thank You for desiring that intimate relationship with me. Help me to delight in You always, my beloved Father. *Amen.*

Apply

① Read Psalm 147:10–11, Psalm 149:4, Proverbs 11:20 and Isaiah 65:19. Who does God delight in and what does that mean for you personally?

② Read Psalm 37:3–6. What could help you to delight more in the Lord?

Day 9

"He loves us
and delights in us."

Comfort Zone

Day 10

Key Verse

She [Hagar] gave this name to the Lord who spoke to her: 'You are the God who sees me,' for she said, 'I have now seen the One who sees me.

Genesis 16:13 NIV

Reading

Now Sarai, Abram's wife, had borne him no children. But she had an Egyptian slave named Hagar; so she said to Abram, 'The Lord has kept me from having children. Go, sleep with my slave; perhaps I can build a family through her.'

Abram agreed to what Sarai said. So after Abram had been living in Canaan ten years, Sarai his wife took her Egyptian slave Hagar and gave her to her husband to be his wife. He slept with Hagar, and she conceived.

When she knew she was pregnant, she began to despise her mistress. Then Sarai said to Abram, 'You are responsible for the wrong I am suffering. I put my slave in your arms, and now that she knows she is pregnant, she despises me. May the Lord judge between you and me.'

The God Who Sees Me

'Your slave is in your hands,' Abram said. 'Do with her whatever you think best.' Then Sarai mistreated Hagar; so she fled from her.

The angel of the Lord found Hagar near a spring in the desert; it was the spring that is beside the road to Shur. And he said, 'Hagar, slave of Sarai, where have you come from, and where are you going?'

'I'm running away from my mistress Sarai,' she answered.

Then the angel of the Lord told her, 'Go back to your mistress and submit to her.' The angel added, 'I will increase your descendants so much that they will be too numerous to count.'

The angel of the Lord also said to her:

*'You are now pregnant
and you will give birth to a son.
You shall name him Ishmael,
for the Lord has heard of your misery' ...*

She gave this name to the Lord who spoke to her: 'You are the God who sees me,' for she said, 'I have now seen the One who sees me.'

Genesis 16:1–11,13 NIV

Reflect

The phrase 'I see you' has become popular in recent times. Its meaning depends on the context, but it's often used as a phrase of encouragement or validation. 'I see what you're going through. I accept you for who you are.' Like any catchphrase, however, it can sometimes be used as a throwaway comment. Someone might say they 'see me', but do they really understand what I'm going through?

Hagar, the Egyptian maidservant of Sarai, found herself alone and in a desperate situation. As Sarai had been unable to bear children, she offered Hagar to her husband Abram so that Sarai could have children through her. This may sound strange to us, but it wasn't unusual for the surrounding culture at the time. Hagar became pregnant with Abram's child, but the plan backfired. Hagar despised her mistress, Sarai mistreated her servant, and Hagar subsequently fled.

Pregnant and alone, Hagar must have despaired of her future. But the angel of the Lord came to her and told her to return and submit to her mistress. *'You will have a son,'* the angel said. *'You shall name him Ishmael, for the Lord has heard of your misery'* (Genesis 16:11 NIV)

'Ishmael' literally means 'God hears'.

Imagine her amazement as she spoke, *'You are the God who sees me.'* God knew what Hagar was going through, and He had a future for both her son and her.

We never have to wonder if God knows our situation or cares for us. He is still the God who sees us.

Pray

Dear Lord, thank You that You see everything I'm going through and that You care for me and my future. Help me to see You in every situation. *Amen.*

Apply

① Think of a time when you've been 'seen' or 'unseen' by those around you. How did you feel in those situations?

② The angel of the Lord came to Hagar near a spring in the desert. It was subsequently called 'Beer Lahai Roi' (Genesis 16:14) which means 'well of the Living One who sees me'. What does it mean to you to know that God sees you in your desert times?

Comfort Zone

Day 11

Key Verse

Depart from me, all you workers of evil, for the Lord has heard the sound of my weeping.

Psalm 6:8 ESV

Reading

And [Sarah] said, 'Who would have said to Abraham that Sarah would nurse children? Yet I have borne him a son in his old age.'

And the child grew and was weaned. And Abraham made a great feast on the day that Isaac was weaned. But Sarah saw the son of Hagar the Egyptian, whom she had borne to Abraham, laughing. So she said to Abraham, 'Cast out this slave woman with her son, for the son of this slave woman shall not be heir with my son Isaac.'

And the thing was very displeasing to Abraham on account of his son. But God said to Abraham, 'Be not displeased because of the boy and because of your slave woman. Whatever Sarah says to you, do as she tells you, for through Isaac shall your offspring be named. And I will make a nation of the son of the slave woman also, because he is your offspring.'

Day 11

The God Who Hears Me

So Abraham rose early in the morning and took bread and a skin of water and gave it to Hagar, putting it on her shoulder, along with the child, and sent her away. And she departed and wandered in the wilderness of Beersheba.

When the water in the skin was gone, she put the child under one of the bushes. Then she went and sat down opposite him a good way off, about the distance of a bowshot, for she said, 'Let me not look on the death of the child.' And as she sat opposite him, she lifted up her voice and wept.

And God heard the voice of the boy, and the angel of God called to Hagar from heaven and said to her, 'What troubles you, Hagar? Fear not, for God has heard the voice of the boy where he is. Up! Lift up the boy, and hold him fast with your hand, for I will make him into a great nation.' Then God opened her eyes, and she saw a well of water. And she went and filled the skin with water and gave the boy a drink. And God was with the boy, and he grew up.

Genesis 21:7–20a ESV

Reflect

The phrase 'I hear you' has also been popular in recent years. Again, it depends on the context, but it is often used when someone agrees with you, especially if they can relate to what you're saying. You tell them things are difficult and they say, 'Oh, I hear you', but do they really? They might just mean they've got problems too.

In yesterday's devotion, we read that God had heard of Hagar's misery and that she was to name her son Ishmael, which means *God hears* (Genesis 16:11). Today's scripture passage takes place some years later. Sarai, now named Sarah, has given birth to Isaac, the son whom God had promised. But when she sees that Hagar's son is laughing, she asks Abraham to get rid of Hagar and Ishmael.

When they ran out of water in the desert, Hagar wept as she waited for what she thought would be the death of her son. But the Angel of the Lord called to her and said, *'What troubles you, Hagar? Fear not, for God has heard the voice of the boy where he is. Up! Lift up the boy, and hold him fast with your hand, for I will make him into a great nation'* (Genesis 21:17b-18). God provided water for their physical need, the boy grew to manhood, and God did indeed make him into a great nation. Many people currently living in the Middle East are descended from Ishmael.

God hears you in your distress. He hears your sobs. He hears your groans. Your sorrow is not hidden from Him. He knows what's in your heart. When no one else is listening, He is the God who hears.

Pray

Dear Lord, thank You that You hear the deepest cry of my heart, even when I cry out alone. No matter what I go through in this life, help me to remember that You are the Lord who hears. *Amen.*

Apply

① Think of a time when you felt 'heard' by someone and a time when you felt 'unheard'. Compare how you felt on each of those occasions.

② In Psalm 6, David knows that the Lord has heard his weeping. How does this give him confidence to face his trials?

Comfort Zone

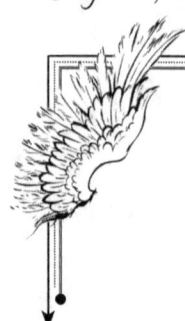

Day 12

Key Verse

She had heard about Jesus, so she came in the crowd behind Him, saying to herself, 'If I just touch His clothes, I will get well.'

Mark 5:27–28 GNT

Reading

As Jesus went along, the people were crowding Him from every side. Among them was a woman who had suffered from severe bleeding for twelve years; she had spent all she had on doctors, but no one had been able to cure her. She came up behind Jesus in the crowd and touched the edge of His cloak, and her bleeding stopped at once. Jesus asked, 'Who touched Me?'

Everyone denied it, and Peter said, 'Master, the people are all around You and crowding in on You.'

But Jesus said, 'Someone touched Me, for I knew it when power went out of Me.'

The woman saw that she had been found out, so she came trembling and threw herself at Jesus' feet.

Day 12

A Touch from the Lord

There in front of everybody, she told Him why she had touched Him and how she had been healed at once. Jesus said to her, 'My daughter, your faith has made you well. Go in peace.'

Luke 8:42b–48 GNT

Reflect

If anyone was in need of a touch from the Lord, it was this woman who had experienced a bleeding disorder for twelve years. She had spent all of her money on doctors but had only gotten worse (Mark 5:26). Such a condition would have left her isolated in Jewish culture, where she would have been regarded as unclean for as long as the discharge lasted. Even someone who touched her would be regarded as unclean (see Leviticus 15:25–30). Can you imagine being in that situation for twelve years?

When she heard that Jesus was nearby, she was desperate. This might be her last chance for healing. She couldn't approach Him and expect Him to touch her in her unclean state, but she knew she would be healed if she even touched the hem of His garment. As soon as she touched Jesus' robe, she instantly felt healing in her body (Mark 5:29).

Jesus was on His way to important business, having been summoned to heal the daughter of a Jewish leader. He didn't have to stop. The woman had been healed and He could have kept moving with the crowd. But He had more than physical healing in mind. He asked who'd touched Him and eventually the trembling woman came and confessed. Would Jesus rebuke her for making Him ceremonially unclean? No, indeed. He called her 'daughter', and made sure that the whole crowd knew the woman had been healed of her suffering. Not only was she healed physically, but she was restored to community.

Do you need a touch from the Lord today? Reach out to Jesus, knowing that He cares about all aspects of your being, not just the physical.

Pray

Dear Lord, thank You that You care about every part of me. As I reach out to You, please let me feel Your healing touch today. *Amen*.

Day 12

Apply

① Read Mark 1:40–45, which recounts Jesus' healing of a man with leprosy. People with skin diseases were also regarded as unclean in Jewish culture (Leviticus 13:1–46). What strikes you most about Jesus' encounter with the leper?

② In which areas of your life do you need a touch from the Lord? Pray now, asking for His help.

He cares about all aspects of your being.

Comfort Zone

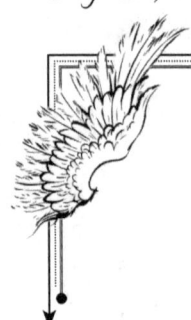

Day 13

Key Verse

Taste and see that the Lord is good.

Psalm 34:8a NLT

Reading

*Taste and see that the Lord is good.
Oh, the joys of those who take refuge in him!
Fear the Lord, you his godly people,
for those who fear him will have all they need.
Even strong young lions sometimes go hungry,
but those who trust in the Lord will lack no good thing.*

Psalm 34:8–10 NLT

Reflect

Have you ever tried a small amount of something to see if you liked it before committing to the whole? These tasters could be something we actually taste, like a spoonful of a new flavour at an ice cream parlour; or it could be a sample of something, such as a free trial of a streaming

Day 13

Tasting the Goodness of God

service or course. The person or organisation offering the 'taste' hopes that you will see how good it is and then buy or subscribe to the whole thing.

Our key verse for today tells us to *'taste and see that the Lord is good.'* We may know people who have many good qualities, but God alone is completely good (Mark 10:18). We may have some good experiences, but every good and perfect gift comes from God (James 1:17). What the world sees as good is sometimes at odds with God's Word, but *'those who trust in the Lord will lack no good thing'* (Psalm 34:10b NLT).

Sadly, some people have tasted Christianity and come to the faulty conclusion that God is not good. They may have known Christians who didn't practise what they preached, or they visited a legalistic church where they felt anything but love. One of my students left her church and her faith because she felt judged and labelled for something she'd done. I've sometimes doubted the goodness of God when prayers I thought were in His will have gone unanswered. None of us is perfect, but if we genuinely seek the Lord, He will reveal more and more of His goodness to us and we can join with the Psalmist in declaring, *'How sweet Your words taste to me; they are sweeter than honey. Your commandments give me understanding'* (Psalm 119:103–104a NLT).

Let's take God up on His challenge. Taste and see for yourself that He is good.

Pray

Dear Lord, thank You that You alone are completely good. Help me to see that Your goodness is not negated by difficulties that come my way, but that You provide me with every good thing that I need. *Amen.*

Apply

① Have you ever doubted the goodness of God because of something that's happened to you? Ask God to give you His perspective on the situation.

② Read 1 Peter 2:1–3. What can you do this week to taste more of God's Word?

Day 13

*Every good
and perfect gift
comes from God.*

Comfort Zone

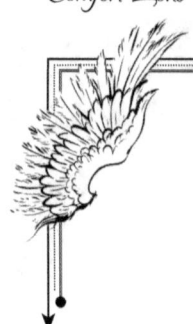

Day 14

Key Verse

My sacrifice is a humble spirit, O God;
You will not reject a humble and repentant heart.

Psalm 51:17 GNT

Reading

In that town was a woman who lived a sinful life. She heard that Jesus was eating in the Pharisee's house, so she brought an alabaster jar full of perfume and stood behind Jesus, by His feet, crying and wetting His feet with her tears. Then she dried His feet with her hair, kissed them, and poured the perfume on them. When the Pharisee saw this, he said to himself, 'If this man really were a prophet, He would know who this woman is who is touching Him; He would know what kind of sinful life she lives!' …

Then [Jesus] turned to the woman and said to Simon, 'Do you see this woman? I came into your home, and you gave me no water for My feet, but she has washed My feet with her tears and dried them with her hair. You did not welcome Me with a kiss, but she has not stopped kissing My feet since I

Day 14

An Aroma Pleasing to God

came. You provided no olive oil for My head, but she has covered My feet with perfume. I tell you, then, the great love she has shown proves that her many sins have been forgiven. But whoever has been forgiven little shows only a little love.'

Then Jesus said to the woman, 'Your sins are forgiven.'

Luke 7:37–39, 44–48 GNT

Reflect

In Old Testament times, burnt offerings were sacrificed to the Lord as a sign of devotion or in order to atone for sin. When sacrifices were genuine and heartfelt, they were regarded as pleasing and acceptable to God. For example, after Noah and his family were saved from a flood that destroyed the rest of humankind, Noah built an altar and sacrificed burnt offerings to the Lord. The Genesis account tells us that *'The Lord smelled the pleasing aroma and said in his heart: "Never again will I curse the ground because of humans"'* (Genesis 8:21a NIV).

However, the religious practices of the wicked were detestable to God. The prophet Amos brought God's word to those who had cast godly behaviour aside and were perpetrating injustices: *'I hate, I despise your religious festivals; your assemblies are a stench to me. Even though you bring me burnt offerings and grain offerings, I will not accept them'* (Amos 5:21–22a NIV).

Consider how Simon the Pharisee would have felt in the episode recounted in our reading today. He was entertaining Jesus, when a sinful woman waltzes in, wets Jesus' feet with her tears, dries His feet and kisses them, then pours perfume all over them. The fact that Jesus let the woman get away with this was surely proof, in Simon's eyes, that He wasn't a prophet at all. Otherwise, He would have known who this woman was and distanced Himself from her. Imagine Simon's surprise when Jesus commends the woman's actions and tells her that her sins are forgiven. Her offering was a sweet-smelling sacrifice to the Lord who would later sacrifice Himself for our sin once and for all.

Let's come to the Lord with humble and repentant hearts, and seek to make our lives worthy of the sacrifice He has freely given for us.

Day 14

Pray

Dear Lord, thank You for all You have sacrificed on my behalf. Help me to live a life that is pleasing to You. *Amen*.

Apply

① Read the full account of the woman's interaction with Jesus in Luke 7:36–50. What strikes you most in that story?

② Read Romans 12:1–2. What can we do to be living sacrifices that are pleasing to God?

The great love she has shown proves that her many sins have been forgiven.

Comfort Zone

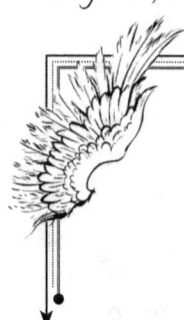

Day 15

Key Verse

[The gifts you sent] are like a sweet-smelling offering to God, a sacrifice which is acceptable and pleasing to Him.

Philippians 4:18b GNT

Reading

But it was very good of you to help me in my troubles. You Philippians know very well that when I left Macedonia in the early days of preaching the Good News, you were the only church to help me; you were the only ones who shared my profits and losses. More than once when I needed help in Thessalonica, you sent it to me. It is not that I just want to receive gifts; rather, I want to see profit added to your account. Here, then, is my receipt for everything you have given me—and it has been more than enough! I have all I need now that Epaphroditus has brought me all your gifts. They are like a sweet-smelling offering to God, a sacrifice which is acceptable and pleasing to Him. And with all His abundant wealth through Christ

Day 15

The Fragrance of Gifts

Jesus, my God will supply all your needs. To our God and Father be the glory forever and ever! Amen.

Philippians 4:14–20 GNT

Reflect

Most of us have probably received gifts for occasions like birthdays or Christmas. There's anticipation as the special day approaches and we can't wait to open the packages and see what's inside. If it's something we like or something we've wanted for a long time, we might be especially delighted. But if we receive an unexpected gift at a time of need, it can be even more meaningful.

Paul wrote his letter to the Philippians when he was in great need. He was being held as a prisoner for defending the gospel. It's not clear whether he was in a prison or under house arrest, but he was in chains (Philippians 1:13) and would have had his freedom severely restricted. He also would have been relying on friends for most of his daily provisions.

How happy he must have been when Epaphroditus arrived with gifts from the church in Philippi. Paul doesn't specify the exact nature of the gifts but says that it was more than enough. There was most likely some money to pay for necessities, and there may have been other practical gifts such as food or clothing. Whatever it was, Paul was greatly encouraged.

Moreover, the gift was like a fragrant offering made to God Himself. Paul didn't just look to the givers of this particular gift, but to the ultimate Gift Giver, the Lord Himself. Not only had God provided what Paul needed, but there was also the assurance that He would supply everything the Philippians needed 'with all His abundant wealth through Christ Jesus' (Philippians 4:19).

Let us always be thankful for the gifts God has given us and look for opportunities to share His blessings with others.

Pray

Dear Lord, thank You for the gift of Your Son and the many material and spiritual gifts You have given me. Please help me to be more aware of the needs around me and look for opportunities to bless others as You have blessed me. *Amen*.

Day 15

Apply

① Read 2 Corinthians 9:6–15. Why should we be generous in our giving?

② Pray and ask God if there is someone who would appreciate a gift from you this week.

The gift was like a fragrant offering made to God Himself.

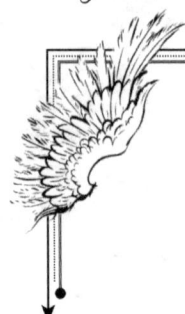

Day 16

Key Verse

Since ancient times no one has heard, no ear has perceived, no eye has seen any God besides You, who acts on behalf of those who wait for Him.

Isaiah 64:4 NIV

Reading

*Oh, that You would rend the heavens and come down,
that the mountains would tremble before You!
As when fire sets twigs ablaze
and causes water to boil,
come down to make Your name known to Your enemies
and cause the nations to quake before You!
For when You did awesome things that we
    did not expect,
You came down, and the mountains trembled
    before You.
Since ancient times no one has heard,
no ear has perceived,
no eye has seen any God besides You,
who acts on behalf of those who wait for Him.*

Isaiah 64:1–4 NIV

The God Who Acts

Reflect

I'd been away from home for almost seven months—first in Melbourne doing a missions course, followed by a nine-week outreach in the United States and Mexico. After ministering in San Diego for a few weeks, we hired a van to take us to Guadalajara for the next leg of our trip. Once we'd left Guadalajara, however, the van kept breaking down. The church we were working with in Mexico City provided other transport for us while there, but we still had to return to the States to catch our international flights back to Australia.

We were in a pickle. The parts needed to fix the van were held up in customs and the hire company wouldn't let us leave the van in Mexico and make other travel arrangements. It was getting closer and closer to our deadline until we no longer had enough time to drive back. We were going to miss our flights. I promptly did what any good missionary would do. I went into my room and cried. As I was pouring out all of my grief and homesickness, I felt God whisper to me.

'If you trust Me, you'll be home in an instant.'

By the next morning, the hire company had given permission for us to leave the van in Mexico and the church had offered to pay our airfares back to the US so we could catch our international flights. When things seemed impossible, God was working behind the scenes in ways we couldn't comprehend. The Bible is full of examples of God acting on behalf of those who *'wait'* for Him. In the original Hebrew, *waiting* is not just sitting around until something happens. It means *awaiting* or *longing* for something or someone.

During our times of waiting, let's put our trust in the One who acts on our behalf.

Pray

Dear Lord, thank You for always acting in our best interests. Help us to focus on You and trust You, even when we can't see what You're doing behind the scenes. *Amen*.

Day 16

Apply

① Paul quotes from Isaiah in 1 Corinthians 2:9–10, though the wording is a little different. How do those verses shed more light on God's work?

② Do you need God to intervene in a current situation? What can you do while waiting?

> God was working behind the scenes in ways we couldn't comprehend.

Comfort Zone

Day 17

Key Verse

Look at the birds. They don't plant or harvest or store food in barns, for your heavenly Father feeds them. And aren't you far more valuable to Him than they are?

Matthew 6:26 NLT

Reading

'That is why I tell you not to worry about everyday life—whether you have enough food and drink, or enough clothes to wear. Isn't life more than food, and your body more than clothing? Look at the birds. They don't plant or harvest or store food in barns, for your heavenly Father feeds them. And aren't you far more valuable to Him than they are? Can all your worries add a single moment to your life?

'And why worry about your clothing? Look at the lilies of the field and how they grow. They don't work or make their clothing, yet Solomon in all his glory was not dressed as beautifully as they are. And if God cares so wonderfully for wildflowers that are here

God Cares for Your Needs

today and thrown into the fire tomorrow, He will certainly care for you. Why do you have so little faith?

'So don't worry about these things, saying, "What will we eat? What will we drink? What will we wear?" These things dominate the thoughts of unbelievers, but your heavenly Father already knows all your needs. Seek the Kingdom of God above all else, and live righteously, and He will give you everything you need.

'So don't worry about tomorrow, for tomorrow will bring its own worries. Today's trouble is enough for today.'

Matthew 6:25–34 NLT

Reflect

One of my friends was a missionary with a student group on the campus where I worked. When I was praying one day, I felt God prompting me to give her $30. My first thought was, 'I can give her more than that. I can give her $40 or $50.' Yet I felt God affirm that $30 was the right amount.

A couple of days later, I saw my friend talking to another young woman on campus. I quickly went back to my office, put the money into an envelope with a brief note, and went back to the spot where I'd seen her. I intended to hand the envelope to her discreetly and then leave so that I didn't interrupt her conversation, but she asked me to stay while she opened it.

Her eyes lit up. 'I have to pay a bill for $38 this afternoon,' she said, 'and I only have $8 in my purse.'

That $8 plus my $30 was of course the exact money she needed. I was blown away. If I had given her $40 or $50, it would have still blessed her and she would have had a little extra after paying her bill, but God knew precisely what she needed.

As I write this, there is a cost-of-living crisis in full swing and many people are having trouble making ends meet. In many countries, the needs are dire. But we have the promise that if we seek Him first, He will take care of our needs. What can you trust Him with today?

Pray

Dear Lord, thank You that You know my needs even before I ask. Please help me to keep my eyes on You and trust in Your provision. *Amen.*

Apply

① (a) What things do you most need at the moment? Try to be as specific as possible.

(b) Are any of these really wants rather than needs?

② Read Matthew 6:25–34.

(a) What is the relationship between seeking *'first His Kingdom and His righteousness'* and having our needs met (v. 33)?

(b) What specific actions could you take to put God first in your life?

God knew precisely what she needed.

Comfort Zone

Day 18

Key Verse

Do not merely listen to the word, and so deceive yourselves. Do what it says.

James 1:22 NIV

Reading

What good is it, my brothers, if someone says he has faith but does not have works? Can that faith save him? If a brother or sister is poorly clothed and lacking in daily food, and one of you says to them, 'Go in peace, be warmed and filled,' without giving them the things needed for the body, what good is that? So also faith by itself, if it does not have works, is dead.

But someone will say, 'You have faith and I have works.' Show me your faith apart from your works, and I will show you my faith by my works. You believe that God is one; you do well. Even the demons believe—and shudder! Do you want to be shown, you foolish person, that faith apart from works is useless?

James 2:14–20 ESV

Day 18

Helping Others Now

Reflect

I used to be an academic at a large regional university. There was some flexibility in our hours, so I decided to head home early one day. As I was walking to my car, I could see a young woman waving to me in the distance. It turned out that she was a Korean student who had only arrived in town the day before. It was the middle of winter and her orientation was scheduled for the next day.

'Where can I buy a blanket on campus?' she asked.

'There's nowhere on campus to buy a blanket,' I replied. 'You'll have to catch a bus to the shopping centre.'

Her face fell. I could have said goodbye, safe in the knowledge that someone would help her out at orientation. But it was cold now, and she needed that blanket tonight. So I drove her to the shopping centre. She picked out a blanket and got a few other things she needed. By the time I dropped her back at her accommodation and drove home, I was much later than I usually would have been. Leave work early to get home late? The irony wasn't lost on me.

James doesn't mince words with his readers. If someone is in need of food or clothing [or blankets], there's no point telling them to stay warm and be well fed if we don't actually do something to help them. Faith without actions is not really faith at all.

I'd like to say that I'm always helpful to others, but there are many times I've turned a blind eye or rationalised my lack of help in some way. We can't meet every need, but we can help where God leads. Let's aim to be doers of the Word, not just hearers.

Pray

Dear Lord, thank You for the countless ways You've provided for me. Help me to consider the needs of others and help where I can. *Amen.*

Day 18

Apply

① Read Ephesians 2:8–10. We are saved by grace, not by our works. However, God created us to do good works. What might this mean for you personally?

② Read Proverbs 3:27–28. Have you been putting off helping someone when it's within your power to help them? Is there something specific God would have you do right now?

We can help where God leads.

Comfort Zone

Day 19

Key Verse

'I am the good shepherd. The good shepherd lays down His life for the sheep.'

John 10:11 ESV

Reading

'I am the good shepherd. The good shepherd lays down His life for the sheep. He who is a hired hand and not a shepherd, who does not own the sheep, sees the wolf coming and leaves the sheep and flees, and the wolf snatches them and scatters them. He flees because he is a hired hand and cares nothing for the sheep. I am the good shepherd. I know My own and My own know me, just as the Father knows Me and I know the Father; and I lay down My life for the sheep. And I have other sheep that are not of this fold. I must bring them also, and they will listen to My voice. So there will be one flock, one shepherd. For this reason the Father loves Me, because I lay down My life that I may take it up again. No one takes it from Me, but I lay it down of My own accord. I have authority to lay

Jesus the Good Shepherd

Day 19

it down, and I have authority to take it up again. This charge I have received from my Father.'

John 10:11–18 ESV

Reflect

When I was on an outreach in New Zealand, the women on our team were invited to speak to a ladies' group at a country church. It was lambing season, and there was a paddock next to the church with dozens of sheep. I was particularly drawn to a ewe and her two lambs—one was standing up and looking down at the other little fellow who was still on the ground. 'How cute,' I thought and snapped a photo. However, the ewe and larger lamb soon walked away, leaving the other little lamb still on the ground. As it tried to stand up, I could see that something was wrong with its leg. The poor little thing couldn't stand up and was bleating and bleating.

One of the women knew more about farming than me and explained that the mother had rejected it because of its defect. It wouldn't survive unless the farmer hand-reared it, but that was probably unlikely. In the space of a minute, I went from marvelling at the cute little lamb to realising it could die for lack of care.

I don't know for sure what the farmer did with that little lamb, but we don't have to wonder about God's care for us. Jesus is the good shepherd, who looks after His lambs. Our passage for today compares a hired hand to the owner of the sheep. When wolves attack, the hired hand will run away because he cares nothing for the sheep. But Jesus loves us and cares for us so much that He willingly gave up His life for us. Can you imagine a greater love? Let's reaffirm our allegiance to the shepherd of our souls.

Pray

Dear Lord, thank You that You are the good shepherd who cares for us like no other, even giving Your life for us. Please guide me and help me to follow You in all that I do. *Amen*.

Day 19

Apply

① Spend some time meditating on 1 Peter 2:22–25, which highlights what Jesus has done for us. What strikes you most about that passage?

② Read Psalm 23. What does it mean for us to know that the Lord is our shepherd?

Can you imagine a greater love?

Comfort Zone

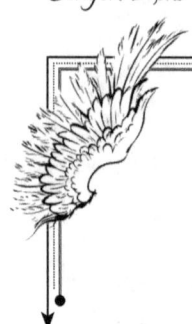

Day 20

Key Verse

Our High Priest is not one who cannot feel sympathy for our weaknesses. On the contrary, we have a High Priest who was tempted in every way that we are, but did not sin.

Hebrews 4:15 GNT

Reading

Let us, then, hold firmly to the faith we profess. For we have a great High Priest who has gone into the very presence of God—Jesus, the Son of God. Our High Priest is not one who cannot feel sympathy for our weaknesses. On the contrary, we have a High Priest who was tempted in every way that we are, but did not sin. Let us have confidence, then, and approach God's throne, where there is grace. There we will receive mercy and find grace to help us just when we need it.

Hebrews 4:14–16 GNT

A God Who Sympathises

Reflect

I was reading a Christian book that offered some valuable insights into an issue I was facing. When a good friend disclosed that she was going through something similar, I lent her my copy. The only problem was that I like to underline passages when I'm reading a nonfiction book, so that I can find key sections later. I thought it would be nice to buy my friend her own copy, but when I gave it to her, I could see the hesitation in her face. After a few seconds, she asked me if she could continue to read my copy. 'Of course,' I said, but I was puzzled. Why wouldn't she want to read her own? She explained that she liked to see which passages I'd marked because it reminded her that someone had been there before her. She knew she wasn't alone in her struggle and that someone else knew what she was going through.

Although there was some overlap in the issues my friend and I faced, there were also differences. I could certainly be sympathetic towards her, but I couldn't know exactly what she was feeling. Fortunately, we have a God who does know exactly what we're thinking and feeling. Jesus can sympathise with us in all our weaknesses because He's been there. He's been rejected. He's been falsely accused. He's suffered incredible pain. He's wept. He's experienced anguish so intense that He's sweated drops of blood (Luke 22:44).

The Greek word translated as *'sympathise'* in our key verse can also mean *to commiserate, to have compassion, to be touched with a feeling*. Whatever you're going through, He understands and has compassion on you.

Pray

Dear Lord, thank You that You chose to come in the flesh and walk on Earth, experiencing our struggles and pain. When I feel like no one else understands what I'm going through, You are there beside me. *Amen*.

Day 20

Apply

① Read Hebrews 4:14–16 again. Why can we approach God's throne with confidence?

② Read Philippians 2:5–11. Why was it important for Jesus to come in human form? What does this show about His compassion for us?

> Jesus can sympathise with us in all our weaknesses because He's been there.

 *Comfort Zone*

Day 21

Key Verse

You have taken account of my wanderings;
Put my tears in Your bottle.
Are they not recorded in Your book?

Psalm 56:8 AMP

Reading

All day long [my enemies] twist my words and say
  hurtful things;
All their thoughts are against me for evil.
They attack, they hide and lurk,
They watch my steps,
As they have [expectantly] waited to take my life.
Cast them out because of their wickedness.
In anger bring down the peoples, O God!
You have taken account of my wanderings;
Put my tears in Your bottle.
Are they not recorded in Your book?
Then my enemies will turn back in the day when I call;
This I know, that God is for me.

Psalm 56:5–9 AMP

Tears in a Bottle

Reflect

We used to own a beautiful little cavoodle named Holly and I'm writing this devotion on what would have been her tenth birthday. A year ago, she was unexpectedly diagnosed with an aggressive rare cancer and died a few weeks later. I have friends who've lost a child and I know that would be a hundred times worse, but I was heartbroken. I cried over that dog every day for the first couple of months and still get teary when I remember her.

I think one of the reasons I was so sad at losing my dog was that she was a real companion and source of comfort. When she was suddenly gone, a lot of other issues bubbled to the surface and I began grieving various losses I'd had over the years, such as never being able to meet my birthmother and not having my own children.

Have you cried buckets of tears over someone or something? Maybe you've lost a beloved family member. Perhaps you've lost your job or had a financial downturn. Maybe you've lost your home, possessions or reputation. Perhaps you've been bullied or misunderstood.

No matter what you've gone through, God is there. He sees your tears. Not only that, but He keeps a record of them. He knows every time you've cried. He saw Hannah's tears as she prayed for a child (1 Samuel 1); He saw Esther weeping at the feet of the king as she pleaded for the lives of her people (Esther 8:3); and He saw the tears that David recorded in our reading for today.

He sees everything that breaks your heart. Trust Him with your tears and let Him heal your wounded heart.

Pray

Dear Lord, thank You that even when I am crying alone, You are right there with me. Thank You that I can draw on Your comfort in times of sorrow. *Amen.*

Day 21

Apply

① The preamble to Psalm 56 tells us that it relates to a time when the Philistines had captured David in Gath. Read through the whole psalm.

  (a) Why was David in anguish?

  (b) Why could he still praise the Lord?

② What does it mean to you to know that God sees your tears and keeps a record of each one?

Trust Him with your tears.

Comfort Zone

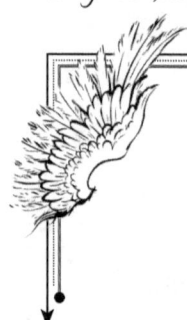

Day 22

Key Verse

And I will ask the Father, and He will give you another Helper, to be with you forever, even the Spirit of truth.

John 14:16–17a ESV

Reading

And I will ask the Father, and He will give you another Helper, to be with you forever, even the Spirit of truth, whom the world cannot receive, because it neither sees Him nor knows Him. You know Him, for He dwells with you and will be in you. I will not leave you as orphans; I will come to you.

John 14:16–18 ESV

Reflect

I was still living with my parents when I attended the university in my home city, but many of my closest friends were from out of town and lived on campus. I spent a lot of time studying with them,

Day 22

The Holy Spirit, Our Comforter

visiting them, going to their parties, and even holidaying with them. The only problem was that when we finished our degrees, they all returned to their own towns.

I was feeling utterly alone one day, when I half-heartedly opened my Bible. The very first verse I laid eyes on was John 16:32 GNT—*'The time is coming, and is already here, when all of you will be scattered, each of you to your own home, and I will be left all alone. But I am not really alone, because the Father is with Me.'* Jesus said these words to the disciples, but it was as if He was speaking directly into my situation. I promptly burst into tears. Jesus understood. The Holy Spirit had brought that verse to my attention to comfort me.

Jesus knew that the disciples were grieving because of His impending departure, but He promised to send them the Holy Spirit who would be with them forever. The word used to describe the Holy Spirit in John 14:16 and 16:7 is 'parakletos', which has been translated in various Bible versions as comforter, helper, advocate, counsellor, and other similar terms. It conveys the sense of someone coming alongside you to help.

Before long, God brought other wonderful friends into my life, but I never forgot the special touch of His Holy Spirit that day. No matter what you're going through, you have a comforter, a counsellor and an advocate to help you through.

Pray

Lord, thank You for giving me the gift of Your Holy Spirit. Help me to draw on His comfort in times of need. *Amen.*

Apply

① Read John 16:7–15. Why was it a good thing that Jesus would be leaving the disciples to return to the Father?

② In John 14:18, Jesus told the disciples He would not leave them as orphans (sometimes translated as *desolate* or *comfortless*). In what way does the gift of the Holy Spirit fulfil this promise?

Day 22

I am not really alone, because the Holy Spirit is with me.

Comfort Zone

Day 23

Key Verse

We do not know what we ought to pray for, but the Spirit Himself intercedes for us through wordless groans.

Romans 8:26b NIV

Reading

We know that the whole creation has been groaning as in the pains of childbirth right up to the present time. Not only so, but we ourselves, who have the firstfruits of the Spirit, groan inwardly as we wait eagerly for our adoption to sonship, the redemption of our bodies. For in this hope we were saved. But hope that is seen is no hope at all. Who hopes for what they already have? But if we hope for what we do not yet have, we wait for it patiently. In the same way, the Spirit helps us in our weakness. We do not know what we ought to pray for, but the Spirit Himself intercedes for us through wordless groans. And He who searches our hearts knows the mind of the Spirit, because the Spirit intercedes for God's people in accordance with the will of God.

Romans 8:22–27 NIV

Day 23

A God Who Intercedes

Reflect

My husband and I spent twelve years trying to have a child, including several in-vitro fertilisation procedures. By the time we neared the end of that journey, I was in my late forties and my husband was in his mid-fifties. As much as I wanted a child, I was starting to wonder if it was a good idea. How would two middle-aged parents cope with a toddler? Was it fair to the child to have such old parents? Was I putting the child at risk of health issues because of my age?

I was no longer sure what to pray, so I said something like, 'Please Lord, help us to have a baby if it would be good for us and the child.' When our last attempt was unsuccessful, I still didn't know how to pray. I felt God was saying to have faith, but did that mean to have faith that we would have a child or to have faith that God was working things for our good even if we didn't have children?

Thanks be to God that the effectiveness of our prayers isn't dependent on our understanding or our brilliant words. The Holy Spirit intercedes on our behalf in words that we can't even express.

Unlike our sometimes flawed or faltering prayers, His prayers are perfect because He prays in accordance with the Father's will.

Not only is the Holy Spirit in our prayer corner, but Jesus is also interceding for us before the very throne of God (Romans 8:34; Hebrews 7:25). May we keep praying in faith, knowing that we have a God who not only hears our prayers, but is actively interceding for us.

Pray

Dear Lord, what a privilege it is to know that You are interceding for me. Thank You that I can pray to You in faith, knowing that You will take my prayers and shape them according to Your will. *Amen.*

Day 23

Apply

① Read Romans 8:22–27, 34 and Hebrews 7:25. What does it mean to you to know that Jesus and the Holy Spirit are interceding on your behalf?

② Bring your prayer requests to God right now, knowing that He hears you and shapes your words into something beautiful for His glory.

God not only hears our prayers, but is actively interceding for us.

Comfort Zone

Day 24

Key Verse

My little children, I am writing these things to you so that you may not sin. But if anyone does sin, we have an advocate with the Father, Jesus Christ the righteous.

1 John 2:1 ESV

Reading

Then Esther spoke to the king again, throwing herself at his feet and crying. She begged him to do something to stop the evil plot that Haman, the descendant of Agag, had made against the Jews. The king held out the gold scepter to her, so she stood up and said, 'If it please Your Majesty, and if you care about me and if it seems right to you, please issue a proclamation to keep Haman's orders from being carried out—those orders that the son of Hammedatha the descendant of Agag gave for the destruction of all the Jews in the empire. How can I endure it if this disaster comes on my people, and my own relatives are killed?'

Day 24

Be an Advocate

King Xerxes then said to Queen Esther and Mordecai, the Jew, 'Look, I have hanged Haman for his plot against the Jews, and I have given Esther his property. But a proclamation issued in the king's name and stamped with the royal seal cannot be revoked. You may, however, write to the Jews whatever you like; and you may write it in my name and stamp it with the royal seal.'

Esther 8:3–8 GNT

Reflect

In my job as a university academic, I once had to submit the name of our top student for a national prize. A colleague objected to the proposed winner one year because the student had been given extensions and he thought the prize should go to someone who had completed within the usual timeframe. A majority of staff agreed with him and a new policy was adopted. However, this was unjust, as the student had been extremely ill and was eligible for the extensions she'd received. Besides, the national body had set the rules and they allowed for extra time. I took my case to the Head of Department, the new policy was overturned and the student received her prize.

Queen Esther risked much more than disapproval from colleagues. She could have been put to death for appearing before the king without being summoned. However, she boldly stood before King Xerxes on behalf of her people. Haman had convinced the king to issue a decree to destroy the Jews (see Esther 3:8–11). However, after Haman's downfall, Esther begged the king to overturn the unjust decree and save her people. The king could not revoke the order already given, but he allowed a proclamation to go out saying that the Jews could defend themselves. They subsequently triumphed over their enemies and were saved (see Esther 9).

Most of us won't have the opportunity to appear before world leaders to plead our case. However, we can stand up for unfairness and injustice where we see it. Just as Jesus is our advocate before the Father, let us advocate for those in need.

Day 24

Pray

Lord Jesus, I will never know how many times you have advocated before the Father's throne on my behalf. Please help me to advocate for those you bring across my path. *Amen*.

Apply

① Read 1 Timothy 2:5 and our key verse. What does it mean to you to know that Jesus advocates to the Father on your behalf?

② Ask God to show you how you could be an advocate for someone in need. For example, defending a friend against unfair criticism or gossip, helping someone to appeal an unfair decision, writing a blog post or letter that calls for justice in a particular situation.

Comfort Zone

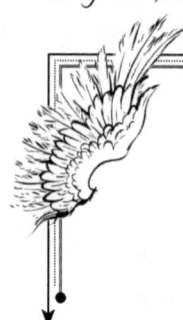

Day 25

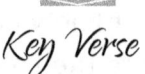

Key Verse

For You created my innermost parts; You wove me in my mother's womb. I will give thanks to You, because I am awesomely and wonderfully made.

Psalm 139:13–14a NASB

Reading

For You created my innermost parts;
You wove me in my mother's womb.
I will give thanks to You, because I am awesomely
*   and wonderfully made;*
Wonderful are Your works, and my soul knows it
*   very well.*
My frame was not hidden from You when I was
*   made in secret,*
And skilfully formed in the depths of the earth;
Your eyes have seen my formless substance;
And in Your book were written
All the days that were ordained for me,
When as yet there was not one of them.

Psalm 139:13–16 NASB

Day 25

God, Our Creator

Reflect

My husband Tim has cerebral palsy, a condition that mainly affects his legs and mobility. He was a premature baby, and it's unclear whether his medical condition was already present in the womb or whether his motor cortex was damaged during a forceps delivery. I know many others who were born with disabilities or health conditions. I was the result of an unplanned pregnancy. Other friends have had miscarriages or lost a baby soon after birth.

When we hear of circumstances like these, it's easy to think that God has taken His eyes off the ball for a minute and an error was made. We live in a fallen world where sickness and other challenges do occur, but that doesn't mean God has somehow lost control. God knows us intimately. He is the one who formed us in the womb.

I love the way the Amplified version translates verse 15: 'My frame was not hidden from You, when I was being formed in secret, and intricately and skillfully formed [as if embroidered with many colours] in the depths of the earth.' That conjures up an image of a loving Creator who took great pride in us, carefully selecting each component that made us who we are. We are not mistakes. We are not Plan B. He was with us in the womb and knew what we would become. Jeremiah 1:4–5 goes even further and says that He knew us before he formed us in the womb.

If you're struggling with your health, appearance, genetic predispositions, identity issues or anything that makes you feel second-best, know this. Father God, your Creator, sees the beauty in you. He fashioned you for His purposes and you are His beloved child.

Pray

Dear Lord, thank You that You formed every part of me and You delighted in Your creation. Help me to see myself through Your eyes and help me to become all that You created me to be. *Amen*.

Day 25

Apply

① Read Psalm 139:13–16 in a few different Bible translations and let the words sink into your soul. What strikes you most about this passage?

② Read Jeremiah 1:4–5. What does it mean for you to realise that God knew you and called you even before He formed you in the womb?

He fashioned you for His purposes and you are His beloved child.

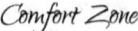
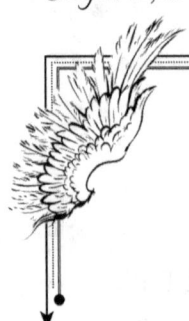

Day 26

Key Verse

So God created man in His own image, in the image of God He created him; male and female He created them.

Genesis 1:27 NASB

Reading

Then God said, 'Let Us make mankind in Our image, according to Our likeness; and let them rule over the fish of the sea and over the birds of the sky and over the livestock and over all the earth, and over every crawling thing that crawls on the earth.' So God created man in His own image, in the image of God He created him; male and female He created them.

Genesis 1:26–27 NASB

Day 26

Made in His Image

Reflect

I was stopped at some traffic lights one day, when I saw two women walking across the road in front of me. I had never seen them before, yet they were clearly mother and daughter. One was probably in her thirties and the other late fifties. They looked alike. They had similar facial expressions and gestures. They were in an animated conversation and clearly had a close relationship. The daughter was the image of her mother.

Though we may bear a resemblance to our earthly parents, today's reading shines a light on something even more remarkable. We are made in the image of God. We are made in His likeness. This is not so much a physical likeness, as a spiritual and moral one. God has placed something of His very essence in us and we are meant to be image-bearers, reflecting His light to our world.

Of course, we often fall short, but God is at work in us. In 2 Corinthians 3:18 (NIV), Paul says that *'we all, who with unveiled faces contemplate the Lord's glory, are being transformed into His image with ever-increasing glory, which comes from the Lord, who is the Spirit.'* As we seek Him, we will become more like Him in thought, word and deed.

If we accept that we are made in God's image, there is another undeniable conclusion. Other people are also made in His image—not just those we love or those who are 'good', but everyone. Like us, they don't always reflect God's image. Some may behave in ways that seem in direct contradiction to what God desires. Yet He is still their Creator and Redeemer. Let's make it our aim to reflect God more and more in our own lives and to treat others as God's children, made in His image.

Pray

Dear Lord, it's a humbling thought to think that I am made in Your image. Please help me to honour You in all I do and to treat others in a way that recognises their intrinsic value as Your children. *Amen.*

Day 26

Apply

① Read Ephesians 4:22–24 and Colossians 3:9–10. What can we do to become more like God in character?

② Read James 3:7–12. What would help you to see others as God sees them?

> *God has placed something of His very essence in us.*

Comfort Zone

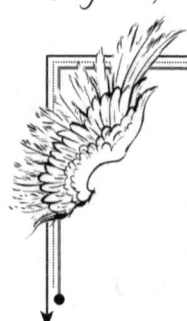

Day 27

Key Verse

And now I give you a new commandment: love one another. As I have loved you, so you must love one another.

John 13:34 GNT

Reading

I may be able to speak the languages of human beings and even of angels, but if I have no love, my speech is no more than a noisy gong or a clanging bell. I may have the gift of inspired preaching; I may have all knowledge and understand all secrets; I may have all the faith needed to move mountains—but if I have no love, I am nothing. I may give away everything I have, and even give up my body to be burned—but if I have no love, this does me no good.

Love is patient and kind; it is not jealous or conceited or proud; love is not ill-mannered or selfish or irritable; love does not keep a record of wrongs; love is not happy with evil, but is happy with the truth. Love never gives up; and its faith, hope, and patience never fail.

Love Others

Love is eternal.

1 Corinthians 13:1–8a GNT

Reflect

Many couples choose the passage of love from 1 Corinthians 13 to be read at their wedding. It exemplifies the best of love and something we would all like to aspire to. Although my husband and I have a happy marriage, God challenged me one day to see these verses in a new light.

If I love my husband, I will be patient and kind. If I love him, I will not be self-seeking. If I love him, I will not keep a record of wrongs. By personalising these and the other statements about love in this passage, I realised how far short I fall. I'm sometimes impatient. I'm sometimes self-seeking. I do sometimes keep a record of wrongs.

Love is not just a feeling that can change depending on our mood or circumstances. We have to desire the best for the other person and seek to show God's love to each other. This kind of love takes commitment, perseverance and work.

None of us is perfect and we will make many mistakes. But if we seek to love others the way God loves us, it can make a difference in their lives as well as our own. Indeed, *'love covers over many sins'* (1 Peter 4:8 GNT).

All the good works in the world will mean nothing if we do not have love (1 Corinthians 13:3). Let us seek to show others the kind of love we've received from God.

Pray

Dear Lord, thank You that You loved me enough to die for my sins and bring me into Your Kingdom. Help me to love others the way that You do, so that they will see You in me. *Amen.*

Day 27

Apply

① Is there anyone in your life at the moment that you find hard to love? How could knowing how much God loves you affect your attitudes and feelings towards this person?

② Personalise 1 Corinthians 13:4–8a and read it out loud. Substitute a particular person's name if relevant (e.g., 'If I love X, I will be patient.').

> *Seek to love others the way God loves us.*

Comfort Zone

Day 28

Key Verse

The man answered, 'You must love the Lord your God with all your heart, all your soul, all your strength, and all your mind.' And, 'Love your neighbour as yourself.'

Luke 10:27 NLT

Reading

One day an expert in religious law stood up to test Jesus by asking Him this question: 'Teacher, what should I do to inherit eternal life?'

Jesus replied, 'What does the law of Moses say? How do you read it?'

The man answered, '"You must love the Lord your God with all your heart, all your soul, all your strength, and all your mind." And, "Love your neighbour as yourself."'

'Right!' Jesus told him. 'Do this and you will live!'

The man wanted to justify his actions, so he asked Jesus, 'And who is my neighbour?'

Day 28

A Good Neighbour

Jesus replied with a story: 'A Jewish man was travelling from Jerusalem down to Jericho, and he was attacked by bandits. They stripped him of his clothes, beat him up, and left him half dead beside the road.

'By chance a priest came along. But when he saw the man lying there, he crossed to the other side of the road and passed him by. A Temple assistant walked over and looked at him lying there, but he also passed by on the other side.

'Then a despised Samaritan came along, and when he saw the man, he felt compassion for him. Going over to him, the Samaritan soothed his wounds with olive oil and wine and bandaged them. Then he put the man on his own donkey and took him to an inn, where he took care of him. The next day he handed the innkeeper two silver coins, telling him, "Take care of this man. If his bill runs higher than this, I'll pay you the next time I'm here."

'Now which of these three would you say was a neighbour to the man who was attacked by bandits?' Jesus asked.

The man replied, 'The one who showed him mercy.'
Then Jesus said, 'Yes, now go and do the same.'

Luke 10:25–37 NLT

Reflect

My husband doesn't have a lot of flexibility in his ankles and knees, which can make it difficult to navigate stairs. When we were on holidays in eastern Canada, I always rang ahead to check whether the accommodation would be suitable, but we sometimes found unexpected obstacles on arrival.

A cottage in Newfoundland only had one step, but it was quite high and the landlord had to help Tim up. Thirty minutes later, he brought us a lower box step he had made in his workshop especially for Tim. One of our stops on Prince Edward Island had wider steps that Tim could use, but no rail. The landlord promptly turned up with carpentry supplies and constructed a railing. At another location, the owner bolted some movable stairs to a post so they wouldn't tip when Tim was climbing them. All of these people went above and beyond what we would have expected, and their help made a big difference.

Many of us would be familiar with the Parable of the Good Samaritan in today's reading. However, the thing that struck me when I reread it was how far the Samaritan went to show compassion to a fellow traveller. He could have easily just

Day 28

dropped the wounded man off at the inn, satisfied that he'd done his bit. But he paid the innkeeper to look after him, and said that he would pay any extra expenses on his return. This is even more remarkable when we learn that Jews and Samaritans usually had nothing to do with each other.

Not all of us can whip up a railing at a moment's notice, but God may sometimes ask us to go above and beyond to help someone. Will we follow when He calls?

Pray

Dear Lord, thank You for the people You've placed in my life to offer help when needed. Please give me a heart to help others as You have helped me. *Amen*.

Apply

① Read the passage from Luke 10:25–37 again and note all of the ways in which the Samaritan provided help.

② What spiritual gifts or practical skills do you have that could help others?

Day 29

Key Verse

Then these righteous ones will reply, 'Lord ... When did we ever see You sick or in prison and visit You?'

And the King will say, 'I tell you the truth, when you did it to one of the least of these my brothers and sisters, you were doing it to Me!'

Matthew 25:37a, 39–40 NLT

Reading

But when the Son of Man comes in His glory, and all the angels with Him, then He will sit upon His glorious throne. All the nations will be gathered in His presence, and He will separate the people as a shepherd separates the sheep from the goats. He will place the sheep at His right hand and the goats at His left.

Then the King will say to those on His right, 'Come, you who are blessed by My Father, inherit the Kingdom prepared for you from the creation of the world. For I was hungry, and you fed Me. I was thirsty, and you gave Me a drink. I was a stranger, and you invited Me into your home. I was naked, and you

Day 29

The Least of These

gave Me clothing. I was sick, and you cared for Me. I was in prison, and you visited Me.'

Then these righteous ones will reply, 'Lord, when did we ever see You hungry and feed You? Or thirsty and give You something to drink? Or a stranger and show You hospitality? Or naked and give You clothing? When did we ever see You sick or in prison and visit You?'

And the King will say, 'I tell you the truth, when you did it to one of the least of these my brothers and sisters, you were doing it to Me!'

Then the King will turn to those on the left and say, 'Away with you, you cursed ones, into the eternal fire prepared for the devil and his demons. For I was hungry, and you didn't feed Me. I was thirsty, and you didn't give Me a drink. I was a stranger, and you didn't invite Me into your home. I was naked, and you didn't give Me clothing. I was sick and in prison, and you didn't visit Me.'

Then they will reply, 'Lord, when did we ever see You hungry or thirsty or a stranger or naked or sick or in prison, and not help You?'

And He will answer, 'I tell you the truth, when you refused to help the least of these my brothers and sisters, you were refusing to help Me.'

Nola Lorraine

And they will go away into eternal punishment, but the righteous will go into eternal life.

Matthew 25:31–46 NLT

Reflect

I never thought I'd find myself performing dramatic plays inside a Mexican jail, but anything can happen when you go on a short-term outreach. We had been given permission to accompany the chaplain into a men's prison in Guadalajara. Security was tight and we had to leave one of our props at check-in. I guess a plastic baseball bat looks like a weapon! Were we about to meet hardened criminals? Were we in danger?

We were led to an area where about forty men from the prison's Christian fellowship were waiting for us. Our group wasn't allowed to interact with them personally, but we could perform our plays and the chaplain could give a message. There were a variety of reactions, but I'll never forget the beaming smiles of some of the inmates. Yes, they had committed crimes and were serving their time, but they had discovered Jesus in prison.

Our reading for today is a challenging one. We're told that whenever we show practical care for

Day 29

those in need—whether they're sick, hungry, thirsty, in prison or in need of clothing—we are actually doing it as if for Jesus. When we withhold our help from the needy, it's as if we're refusing the Lord himself.

I've failed in this area many times, but God is gracious. He longs for us to see others as He sees them and to touch them with His love. Let's be ambassadors of His grace.

Pray

Dear Lord, please forgive me for the times I haven't reflected Your love to those in need. Help me to treat each person in a way that is honouring to You and to meet needs where I can. *Amen.*

Apply

① Read Matthew 25:31–40. Can you think of a time when you had a need and a brother or sister in Christ provided some practical help for you?

② Read Matthew 25:41–46. Pray and ask God if there is something you could do to help someone in need this week.

Comfort Zone

Day 30

Key Verse

*He will cover you with His feathers,
and under His wings you will find refuge;
His faithfulness will be your shield and rampart.*

Psalm 91:4 NIV

Reading

*Whoever dwells in the shelter of the Most High
will rest in the shadow of the Almighty.
I will say of the Lord, 'He is my refuge and my fortress,
my God, in whom I trust.'
Surely He will save you
from the fowler's snare
and from the deadly pestilence.
He will cover you with His feathers,
and under His wings you will find refuge;
His faithfulness will be your shield and rampart.*

Psalm 91:1–4 NIV

Day 30

A God of Refuge

Reflect

We were visiting a friend in a rural area in New Zealand. As we turned into her long driveway, we saw a quail hen and her little chicks right in front of us. I stopped the car and, in a matter of seconds, the hen pulled the ten or so chicks to herself so that they were all completely covered by her wings. If I hadn't seen it with my own eyes, I would have assumed it was just a fat little hen by herself. She wasn't budging, so I had to get out of the car and walk up to my friend's house.

I love the image of God we have in today's psalm. Like that hen who was fiercely protective of her chicks, God is our sure refuge. He is our shield against the arrows of the enemy (Ephesians 6:16). He is our rampart, or defensive wall, against attack. He provides rest for those who come under His shelter.

It's so easy to make other things our refuge—money and possessions, career or success, addictions, other people. Comfort food has been one of my big ones. There's nothing that can't be solved by a kilo of chocolate and a jumbo-sized packet of chips. Or is there?

We may find temporary relief in such things, but it doesn't last. We can lose money and possessions in an instant, addictions create more cravings so that we are never satisfied, people will let us down. But God is constant. If we make Him our refuge, we have nothing to fear from the enemy. Let's choose the cover of His wings rather than the false refuges that vie for our allegiance.

Pray

Dear Lord, forgive me for the times I've sought refuge in things and people apart from You. Thank You that You are my sure refuge. May I always shelter under Your wings. *Amen*.

Day 30

Apply

① What are some things that you've taken refuge in? Have any of these things given you a false sense of security or taken you away from God?

② Read Psalm 46. Why can we trust in God as our refuge?

If we make Him our refuge, we have nothing to fear from the enemy.

Comfort Zone

Day 31

Key Verse

God, the Lord, is my strength; He makes my feet like the deer's; He makes me tread on my high places.

Habakkuk 3:19 ESV

Reading

Though the fig tree should not blossom, nor fruit be on the vines, the produce of the olive fail and the fields yield no food, the flock be cut off from the fold and there be no herd in the stalls, yet I will rejoice in the Lord; I will take joy in the God of my salvation. God, the Lord, is my strength; He makes my feet like the deer's; He makes me tread on my high places.

Habakkuk 3:17–19 ESV

Reflect

I was on a day trip in the scenic Blue Mountains with two friends. We hopped off the tour bus at a spot that promised a cliffside walk, though it was

Walking on the Heights

more of a mountain trail. A young woman had headed into the bush before us, only to come back a minute later. We found out she was a German tourist who was afraid of heights. The walk looked too scary for her and she had decided to just wait for the next bus.

We convinced her she would be safe if she came with us. I would walk on the outside of the track and she could hold onto my arm. Well, she had my arm in a death grip for the first part of the walk, but gradually relaxed, even letting go of me a couple of times to look at something one of the others was pointing out. At the end, she thanked us and took a photo with us. I'm sure we became one of her holiday anecdotes!

I like the Amplified Bible's translation of today's verse: *'The Lord God is my strength [my source of courage, my invincible army]; He has made my feet [steady and sure] like hind's feet [deer's feet]. And makes me walk [forward with spiritual confidence] on my high places [of challenge and responsibility]!'*

Just as the German tourist wouldn't have tackled that walk without our help, there are many challenges we might hesitate to take on by ourselves. The good news is that God does not expect us to handle difficult situations alone. He is there walking beside us, holding our hand, keeping us safe, helping us to venture out into the paths He has for us. Whatever challenges you face today, know that God is with you every step of the way.

Pray

Dear Lord, thank You that I don't have to fear my high places because You are walking beside me, helping me at every turn. Help me to be ever mindful of Your presence. *Amen.*

Apply

① Read Psalm 18:31–36. How does God help us in difficult times?

② Are you facing a challenge at the moment? What can you do to draw alongside God?

Day 31

I don't have to fear my high places because God is walking beside me.

Comfort Zone

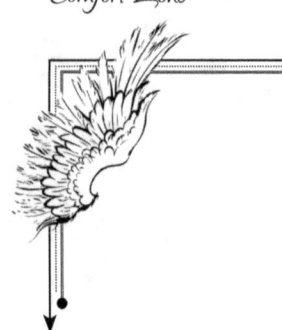

Day 32

Key Verse

But [the Lord] said to me, 'My grace is sufficient for you, for My power is made perfect in weakness.'

2 Corinthians 12:9a ESV

Reading

So to keep me from becoming conceited because of the surpassing greatness of the revelations, a thorn was given me in the flesh, a messenger of Satan to harass me, to keep me from becoming conceited. Three times I pleaded with the Lord about this, that it should leave me. But He said to me, 'My grace is sufficient for you, for My power is made perfect in weakness.' Therefore I will boast all the more gladly of my weaknesses, so that the power of Christ may rest upon me. For the sake of Christ, then, I am content with weaknesses, insults, hardships, persecutions, and calamities. For when I am weak, then I am strong.

2 Corinthians 12:7–10 ESV

Day 32

His Grace is Sufficient

Reflect

I've had a few recurring health issues that sometimes affect my sleep, either because pain makes it difficult for me to find a comfortable position to sleep in or because I'm up and down to the loo through the night. I'm writing this devotion after having a poor night's sleep with both of those issues. It's frustrating because I think how much more I could be doing if I wasn't tired. Have you ever prayed that God would take away some kind of ongoing ailment or problem, yet it still remains? If so, we're in good company.

The Apostle Paul had a thorn in the side that wouldn't go away. We're not told what it was, though commentators have suggested it may have been a physical ailment or continued persecution or opposition. In any case, it was something that tormented him and he pleaded with God three times for its removal. Rather than taking it away, however, God encouraged him by saying that His grace is sufficient because His power is made perfect in weakness. This seems counterintuitive in our society, where strength is seen as an asset. However, it makes perfect sense in God's economy. He works through our weaknesses, so that the glory goes to Him.

This doesn't mean that we shouldn't pray for healing or for God to remove troubles from us. However, it can give us a new perspective in our troubles. We don't have to be strong and rely on ourselves because God is not limited by our weaknesses. Praise God that when we are weak, He is our strength.

Pray

Dear Lord, thank You that You are not limited by my weakness. Help me to know the power of Your strength working through me, and help me to always give the glory to You. *Amen.*

Day 32

Apply

① (a) Read 2 Corinthians 12:1-7. According to Paul, why was he given this thorn in the flesh?

(b) Read Philippians 2:3-4 and 1 Timothy 6:3-5. How should Christ-followers differ from those who follow selfish ambitions?

② Spend some time reflecting on, and praying about, your weaknesses. Ask God to help you see your situation through His perspective. Give Him the glory for what He is doing in and through you.

God is not limited by our weaknesses.

Comfort Zone

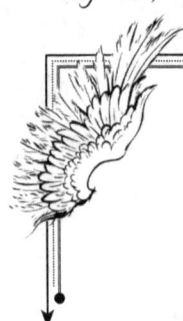

Day 33

Key Verse

Jesus answered, 'His blindness has nothing to do with his sins or his parents' sins. He is blind so that God's power might be seen at work in him.'

John 9:3 GNT

Reading

As Jesus was walking along, he saw a man who had been born blind. His disciples asked him, 'Teacher, whose sin caused him to be born blind? Was it his own or his parents' sin?'

Jesus answered, 'His blindness has nothing to do with his sins or his parents' sins. He is blind so that God's power might be seen at work in him. As long as it is day, we must do the work of him who sent Me; night is coming when no one can work. While I am in the world, I am the light for the world.'

After he said this, Jesus spat on the ground and made some mud with the spittle; He rubbed the mud on the man's eyes and told him, 'Go and wash your face in

Day 33

When it's Not Your Fault

the Pool of Siloam.' (This name means 'Sent.') So the man went, washed his face, and came back seeing.

His neighbours, then, and the people who had seen him begging before this, asked, 'Isn't this the man who used to sit and beg?'

Some said, 'He is the one,' but others said, 'No he isn't; he just looks like him.'

So the man himself said, 'I am the man.'

'How is it that you can now see?' they asked him.

He answered, 'The man called Jesus made some mud, rubbed it on my eyes, and told me to go to Siloam and wash my face. So I went, and as soon as I washed, I could see.'

John 9:1–11 GNT

Reflect

It's easy to sympathise with someone when their troubles are not of their own making, such as a person who loses their home in a natural disaster. However, it's all too easy to point the finger at someone who has an illness, relationship problems, financial difficulties or some other type of problem. We like to believe in a just world, so they must have done something wrong to bring troubles on themselves. God must be punishing them.

Jesus' disciples fell into this trap when they came across a man born blind. They asked him, *'Teacher, whose sin caused him to be born blind? Was it his own or his parents' sin?'* (John 9:2)

Imagine their surprise when Jesus said neither, but that he was blind *'so that God's power might be seen at work in him'* (John 9:3). He then miraculously restored the blind beggar's sight.

Now sometimes we do share in the responsibility for our troubles, and we'll look at that tomorrow, but we live in a fallen world where there is sickness, death and all manner of strife. Sometimes bad things happen through no fault of our own. However, we can choose how we respond to those problems. Do we trust that God can still work through them or do we doubt God's care? I know I've been guilty of the latter at times.

God's compassion doesn't fail or run out. Let's trust in His all-consuming love in spite of our troubles.

Day 33

Pray

Dear Lord, I don't always understand why difficulties and challenges have come into my life, but I know that Your love never fails. Thank You that You are at work in my life. Please help me to reflect Your love to those around me for Your glory. *Amen*.

Apply

① Read John 9:1–11 again. In what way is the work of God being shown in your life, in spite of any difficulties you might be facing?

② In John 9:5, Jesus says, 'While I am in the world, I am the light for the world.' Jesus brought light to the man's eyes by physically healing him of his blindness, but what does this verse mean for those who are spiritually blind?

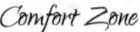

Day 34

Key Verse

Because of Your wrath there is no health in my body; there is no soundness in my bones because of my sin.

Psalm 38:3 NIV

Reading

Miriam and Aaron began to talk against Moses because of his Cushite wife, for he had married a Cushite. 'Has the Lord spoken only through Moses?' they asked. 'Hasn't He also spoken through us?' And the Lord heard this.

(Now Moses was a very humble man, more humble than anyone else on the face of the earth.)

At once the Lord said to Moses, Aaron and Miriam, 'Come out to the tent of meeting, all three of you.' So the three of them went out. Then the Lord came down in a pillar of cloud; He stood at the entrance to the tent and summoned Aaron and Miriam. When the two of them stepped forward, He said, 'Listen to My words:

Day 34

When the Fault Lies with You

*'When there is a prophet among you,
I, the Lord, reveal Myself to them in visions,
I speak to them in dreams.
But this is not true of My servant Moses;
he is faithful in all My house.
With him I speak face to face,
clearly and not in riddles;
he sees the form of the Lord.
Why then were you not afraid
to speak against My servant Moses?'*

The anger of the Lord burned against them, and He left them.

When the cloud lifted from above the tent, Miriam's skin was leprous—it became as white as snow. Aaron turned toward her and saw that she had a defiling skin disease, and he said to Moses, 'Please, my lord, I ask you not to hold against us the sin we have so foolishly committed. Do not let her be like a stillborn infant coming from its mother's womb with its flesh half eaten away.'

So Moses cried out to the Lord, 'Please, God, heal her!'

The Lord replied to Moses, 'If her father had spit in her face, would she not have been in disgrace for seven days? Confine her outside the camp for seven days; after that she can be brought back.' So Miriam was confined outside the camp for seven days, and the people did not move on till she was brought back.

Numbers 12:1–15 NIV

Reflect

Yesterday we saw that difficult circumstances can sometimes befall a person through no fault of their own. However, there are times when our sins or poor choices have contributed to our problems. For example, the person who can't pay their rent because they gambled away their pay or someone who puts their health at risk by smoking or eating lots of junk food.

Moses' sister Miriam put herself at risk through her sin when she and her brother Aaron complained about Moses. *'Has the Lord spoken only through Moses?'* they asked. *'Hasn't he also spoken through us?'* (Numbers 12:2). God had indeed given Miriam a prophetic gift (Exodus 15:20), but here she was guilty of jealousy and spiritual pride. God rebuked Miriam and Aaron for speaking in such a way against Moses,

Day 34

who had been a humble and faithful servant. When God left them, Miriam discovered that her skin had turned white from leprosy.

Aaron sought Moses' forgiveness for both of them. Moses prayed that God would heal her, but first she had to be quarantined outside the camp for a period, as was standard practice for those with infectious skin diseases (see Leviticus 13). That would have given her plenty of time to think about what she'd done and repent of her sin. She'd tried to elevate herself, but was instead brought down to earth. God did heal her and she was restored to the community, with hopefully a different heart attitude.

We all sin from time to time, but God is full of compassion and mercy. If we repent, He will restore us to relationship with Him, but sometimes we still have to walk through the consequences of our bad choices. Let's bring our hearts before Him and ask for His healing, inside and out.

Nola Lorraine

Pray

Dear Lord, I'm sorry for the times I've gone my own way instead of following You. Please show me any area of my life that I need to get right with You and lead me along Your path. *Amen.*

Apply

① Read Galatians 6:7–8. How would you describe the principle of reaping and sowing?

② Read 1 John 1:9 and Psalm 103:11–12. If we confess our sins, what does God promise to do?

Day 34

*If we repent,
God will restore us
to relationship with Him.*

Comfort Zone

Day 35

Key Verse

And we know that in all things God works for the good of those who love Him, who have been called according to His purpose.

Romans 8:28 NIV

Reading

But now that their father was dead, Joseph's brothers became fearful. 'Now Joseph will show his anger and pay us back for all the wrong we did to him,' they said.

So they sent this message to Joseph: 'Before your father died, he instructed us to say to you: "Please forgive your brothers for the great wrong they did to you—for their sin in treating you so cruelly." So we, the servants of the God of your father, beg you to forgive our sin.' When Joseph received the message, he broke down and wept. Then his brothers came and threw themselves down before Joseph. 'Look, we are your slaves!' they said.

But Joseph replied, 'Don't be afraid of me. Am I God, that I can punish you? You intended to harm me, but

Day 35

He Works for Our Good

God intended it all for good. He brought me to this position so I could save the lives of many people. No, don't be afraid. I will continue to take care of you and your children.' So he reassured them by speaking kindly to them.

Genesis 50:15–21 NLT

Reflect

Joseph had every right to be bitter. He was his father's favourite son, yet that caused jealousy among his brothers. Their hatred grew to the point where they threw him into a cistern, sold him to travelling merchants and let their grief-stricken father think that he had died (see Genesis 37).

He was taken to Egypt and experienced many tribulations over the years, including imprisonment. Yet, he maintained his integrity before God and eventually rose to a position of power. When God warned that a devastating famine would follow seven years of plenty, Joseph was put in charge of a program to store up enough grain to sustain Egypt through the lean years.

Imagine the shock and fear of his brothers when they went to Egypt to buy grain and discovered that the brother they had left for dead was still alive and in a position of authority. Now was the time for payback!

However, Joseph didn't retaliate or seek justice for the years he had lost. He recognised that God had brought him to this place for a reason. When his brothers threw themselves down before him, he told them not to be afraid. *'You intended to harm me, but God intended it all for good. He brought me to this position so I could save the lives of many people.'* (Genesis 50:20 NLT) What a testimony!

God is always working for the good of those who belong to Him. This doesn't mean everything that happens to us is good, but that God can bring good out of even the most difficult situations. If you're facing challenges at the moment, take comfort in the knowledge that God is still working for your good.

Day 35

Pray

Dear Lord, it's easy for me to focus on the negative things that are happening in my life, but help me to have Your perspective. Thank You that even in these difficult times, You are working for my good. *Amen*.

Apply

① Read Genesis 50:15–21 again. How is Joseph's response to his brothers different from what we might expect? Why was he able to respond like that?

② Think of an example where you experienced a difficult circumstance and later saw some good come from it. Spend some time thanking God that He is working for your good.

Comfort Zone

Day 36

Key Verse

I will remember the deeds of the Lord;
yes, I will remember Your wonders of old.

Psalm 77:11 ESV

Reading

I cry aloud to God, aloud to God, and He will hear me. In the day of my trouble I seek the Lord; in the night my hand is stretched out without wearying; my soul refuses to be comforted. When I remember God, I moan; when I meditate, my spirit faints …

Then I said, 'I will appeal to this, to the years of the right hand of the Most High.'

I will remember the deeds of the Lord; yes, I will remember Your wonders of old. I will ponder all Your work, and meditate on Your mighty deeds. Your way, O God, is holy. What god is great like our God? You are the God who works wonders; You have made known Your might among the peoples.

Psalm 77:1–3, 10–14 ESV

Day 36

Remembering Past Victories

Reflect

When you're going through a difficult time, it's easy to focus on all the problems of your current situation and forget, or even doubt, all of the things God has done for you in the past. Asaph, the author of Psalm 77, was in that situation. He sought out the Lord in his distress, but says that his soul refused to be comforted (Psalm 77: 2). He wondered if the Lord's unfailing love had vanished, if His compassion was being withheld and if His promise had failed (Psalm 77:8–9).

I can relate to Asaph. My husband and I spent many years trying to have children, yet remained childless. One of the things I found especially difficult was that I felt God had given me a specific promise that we would have children. Why didn't He answer our prayers? Did God renege on his Word?

In spite of Asaph's questions and doubts, he chose to focus on God's goodness. In verses 11 and 12 (ESV), he says: *'I will remember the deeds of the Lord; yes, I will remember Your wonders of old. I will ponder all Your work, and meditate on Your mighty deeds.'* The rest of the Psalm celebrates things that God has done in the past.

Although I still have some questions for God about our childlessness, one of the things that helped me was that I started to keep a daily gratitude journal. Every day, I could think of at least one thing I could be thankful for, sometimes many things. If I ever doubt God's goodness, I can look back over my journal and remember all He has done for me. This fills me with hope for the future. His compassion doesn't stop when we're going through challenging times. We just have to remember.

Pray

Dear Lord, thank You for all of the blessings You have given me over the years. No matter what I'm going through now, help me to always remember Your goodness. *Amen.*

Day 36

Apply

① Read the whole of Psalm 77. Can you relate to some of Asaph's cries? If so, be honest with God about what you're feeling.

② Meditate on verses 11 and 12. What specific activity could you do to help you remember all God has done for you?

> *Be honest with God about what you're feeling.*

Comfort Zone

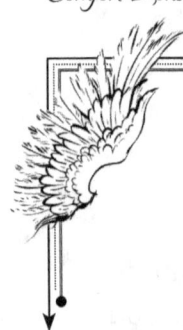

Day 37

Key Verse

Therefore, as God's chosen people, holy and dearly loved, clothe yourselves with compassion, kindness, humility, gentleness and patience.

Colossians 3:12 NIV

Reading

[King David] asked, 'Is there no one still alive from the house of Saul to whom I can show God's kindness?'

Ziba answered the king, 'There is still a son of Jonathan; he is lame in both feet.'

'Where is he?' the king asked.

Ziba answered, 'He is at the house of Makir son of Ammiel in Lo Debar.'

So King David had him brought from Lo Debar, from the house of Makir son of Ammiel. When Mephibosheth son of Jonathan, the son of Saul, came to David, he bowed down to pay him honour.

David said, 'Mephibosheth!'

Ripples of Kindness

'At your service,' he replied.

'Don't be afraid,' David said to him, 'for I will surely show you kindness for the sake of your father Jonathan. I will restore to you all the land that belonged to your grandfather Saul, and you will always eat at my table.'

Mephibosheth bowed down and said, 'What is your servant, that you should notice a dead dog like me?'

Then the king summoned Ziba, Saul's steward, and said to him, 'I have given your master's grandson everything that belonged to Saul and his family. You and your sons and your servants are to farm the land for him and bring in the crops, so that your master's grandson may be provided for. And Mephibosheth, grandson of your master, will always eat at my table.' (Now Ziba had fifteen sons and twenty servants.)

Then Ziba said to the king, 'Your servant will do whatever my lord the king commands his servant to do.' So Mephibosheth ate at David's table like one of the king's sons.

2 Samuel 9:3–11 NIV

Reflect

We don't have to look far to see examples of uncharitable or even malicious behaviour in our world today—the scammer who robs someone of their life savings, the jealous competitor who vilifies you on social media, the colleague who takes all the credit for work you did. Yet there are also countless examples of kindness—the volunteer who helps refugees, the church member who brings a meal when you're sick, the friend who stands by you through thick and thin.

One of the amazing things about kindness is that it has a ripple effect, such that one kind act often leads to another.

King Saul's son Jonathan had shown kindness by warning David of Saul's plot to kill him. On their final morning together, the two friends vowed their allegiance to each other. *'Do not ever cut off your kindness from my family,'* Jonathan begged, and David readily agreed (1 Samuel 20:14–17).

After Saul and Jonathan had both died, David asked, *'Is there anyone still left of the house of Saul to whom I can show kindness for Jonathan's sake?'* (2 Samuel 9:1 NIV)

Saul's steward Ziba told him that Jonathan's son Mephibosheth was still alive. David brought him to Jerusalem and showered him with kindness. He restored to him all the land that belonged to his grandfather Saul, and commissioned Ziba and his family and servants to farm the land so that Mephibosheth would always be provided for. David also treated him like one of his own sons by vowing that Mephibosheth would always eat at the king's table. It may seem like David was being overly extravagant, but it was really the Lord's kindness he was sharing.

A lot of people are going through tough times. You might be one of them. As we reach out with little acts of kindness, we can help reflect God's love to a hurting world.

Pray

Dear Lord, thank You for the extravagant kindness You have shown to us in sending Your Son. Help us to be like lights, reflecting Your kindness to those around us. *Amen*.

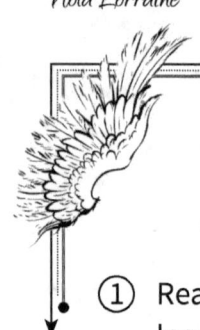

Apply

① Read 1 Samuel 20:10–17; 35–42. What can we learn about kindness from this passage?

② David was intentional about showing kindness. Is there a simple act you could do this week to show kindness to someone?

Day 37

"We can help reflect God's love to a hurting world."

Comfort Zone

Day 38

Key Verse

Keep your lives free from the love of money, and be satisfied with what you have. For God has said, 'I will never leave you; I will never abandon you.'

Hebrews 13:5 GNT

Reading

In view of all this, what can we say? If God is for us, who can be against us? Certainly not God, who did not even keep back His own Son, but offered Him for us all! He gave us His Son—will He not also freely give us all things? Who will accuse God's chosen people? God Himself declares them not guilty! Who, then, will condemn them? Not Christ Jesus, who died, or rather, who was raised to life and is at the right side of God, pleading with Him for us! Who, then, can separate us from the love of Christ? Can trouble do it, or hardship or persecution or hunger or poverty or danger or death? As the Scripture says,

'For Your sake we are in danger of death at all times; we are treated like sheep that are going to
 be slaughtered.'

Day 38

Never Forsaken

No, in all these things we have complete victory through Him who loved us! For I am certain that nothing can separate us from His love: neither death nor life, neither angels nor other heavenly rulers or powers, neither the present nor the future, neither the world above nor the world below—there is nothing in all creation that will ever be able to separate us from the love of God which is ours through Christ Jesus our Lord.

Romans 8:31–39 GNT

Reflect

When my husband Tim and I embarked on a bus trip in Italy, we didn't realise how much walking there would be. This was challenging because Tim's disability affects his mobility. On our first day in Rome, the bus driver dropped us off in front of a busy road. By the time Tim and I got off the bus, the others had crossed the street and were heading off into the distance. A kind truck driver eventually stopped to let us cross, but by then our entire group had disappeared around a corner. My eyes welled with tears. *They didn't even look back. What if we can't find them?*

Imagine my relief when our tour guide, Alberto, appeared around the corner. He hadn't forgotten us. He was just showing the others where they needed to go and had always intended to come back for us. I relaxed a lot more after that, safe in the knowledge that Alberto was looking out for us and wouldn't leave us behind.

People are fallible and sometimes do leave us, either intentionally or because of changing circumstances. But God never changes. He has promised to be with us always. I love the way the Amplified version emphasises the second part of today's verse: *'I will never [under any circumstances] desert you [nor give you up nor leave you without support, nor will I in any degree leave you helpless], nor will I forsake or let you down or relax My hold on you [assuredly not]!'*

Let us rest in the safe arms of our Lord, knowing that He is with us always.

Pray

Dear Lord, though people may come in and out of our lives, You are constant. Thank You that You will never leave me. Just as You will not relax your hold on me, help me to always cling to You. *Amen*.

Apply

① Read Romans 8:31–39. How can you apply those verses to your current situation or a difficult situation you have had in the past?

② Read Matthew 28:16–20. Jesus spoke these words to the disciples before He ascended into heaven. How could He always be with them when He was about to leave them physically? *(See Day 22)*

Comfort Zone

Day 39

Key Verse

'Simon, Simon! Listen! Satan has received permission to test all of you, to separate the good from the bad, as a farmer separates the wheat from the chaff. But I have prayed for you, Simon, that your faith will not fail. And when you turn back to Me, you must strengthen your brothers.'

Luke 22:31–32 GNT

Reading

After they had eaten, Jesus said to Simon Peter, 'Simon son of John, do you love Me more than these others do?'

'Yes, Lord,' he answered, 'You know that I love You.'

Jesus said to him, 'Take care of My lambs.' A second time Jesus said to him, 'Simon son of John, do you love Me?'

'Yes, Lord,' he answered, 'You know that I love You.'

Jesus said to him, 'Take care of My sheep.' A third time Jesus said, 'Simon son of John, do you love Me?'

Day 39

Feed My Sheep

Peter became sad because Jesus asked him the third time, 'Do you love Me?' and so he said to Him, 'Lord, You know everything; You know that I love You!'

Jesus said to him, 'Take care of My sheep.'

John 21:15–17 GNT

Reflect

Have you ever made a promise you couldn't keep? Simon Peter declared that he was ready to go to prison for Jesus and even to die for him (Luke 22:33), yet when Jesus was arrested, fear seized hold of his heart. Just as Jesus had prophesied, Peter denied even knowing his Lord three times before a rooster crowed. When he realised what he had done, Peter wept bitterly (Luke 22:62). How could he be of any use to God after such a monumental fail?

Yet we see in our key verses for today that Jesus had already prayed for Peter and that He still had a task for him to do. When Peter came back to the Lord, He was to strengthen the brothers. After the resurrection, Jesus appeared to the disciples and ate with them. Three times, He asked Peter if he loved Him—one for every denial. Three times, Peter affirmed that he did indeed love the Lord and after each response, Jesus confirmed His commission for him. *'Feed my lambs … take care of my sheep … feed my sheep'* (John 21:15–17).

Peter became one of the leaders of the early church and he is still strengthening us today through the testimonies we read in the Bible and through his own words in the epistles 1 and 2 Peter.

No matter what you've done, no matter how broken you are, no matter how ineffective you feel, God still has a job for you to do. He wants to strengthen you so you can strengthen others. What a privilege to partner with the Lord.

Pray

Dear Lord, I'm sorry for the times I've denied You through my thoughts, words and actions. Help me to take my strength from You, so I can help strengthen others. *Amen.*

Day 39

Apply

① Read Luke 22:54–62 and John 21:15–17. Contrast how Peter would have felt in each scene.

② In what way might Jesus be asking you to strengthen others? What task has He specifically given to you? If you're not sure, pray and ask God to reveal it to you.

> *Peter's legacy is still strengthening us today.*

Comfort Zone

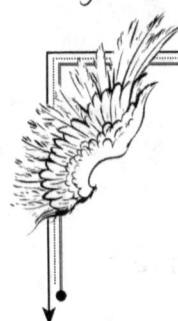

Day 40

Key Verse

*Tears may flow in the night;
but joy comes in the morning.*

Psalm 30:5b GNT

Reading

*I praise You, Lord, because You have saved me
and kept my enemies from gloating over me.
I cried to You for help, O Lord my God,
and You healed me;
You kept me from the grave.
I was on my way to the depths below,
but You restored my life.
Sing praise to the Lord,
all His faithful people!
Remember what the Holy One has done,
and give Him thanks!
His anger lasts only a moment,
His goodness for a lifetime.
Tears may flow in the night,
but joy comes in the morning …
You have changed my sadness into a joyful dance;*

Day 40

Joy in the Morning

*You have taken away my sorrow
and surrounded me with joy.
So I will not be silent;
I will sing praise to You.
Lord, You are my God;
I will give You thanks forever.*

Psalm 30:1–5, 11–12 GNT

Reflect

The disciples believed that Jesus was the Messiah. They had given up everything to follow Him, but now it had all come undone. Judas, one of their own, had betrayed Jesus and handed him over to the Jewish authorities. Jesus' closest friends deserted him in his hour of need. Peter, one of Jesus' most loyal and devoted followers, denied Him three times for fear of his own life. John was apparently the only one of the twelve present at the crucifixion. Jesus' dead body was placed in a sealed tomb. Imagine the anguish of His followers. They had lost their beloved friend.

Jerusalem was still under Roman rule. All hope was gone.

But that's not the end of the story. Jesus' disciples didn't understand that the Messiah had to die for their sins. They didn't realise this was all part of God's plan of salvation. Three days later, Jesus rose from the dead and He appeared to His followers many times over the next few weeks. Imagine their elation. Imagine their unbridled joy.

When we're going through a difficult circumstance, it's not always easy to maintain hope. Yet if we put our trust in Jesus, we can be assured that this season will not last forever. Yes, there is weeping, but joy comes in the morning. We can join with **David and declare:** *'You have changed my sadness into a joyful dance; You have taken away my sorrow and surrounded me with joy. So I will not be silent; I will sing praise to You. Lord, You are my God; I will give You thanks forever'* (**Psalm 30:11–12** GNT).

Whatever your situation today, draw near to the Father of all Comfort, knowing that one day He will wipe away every tear and clothe you in exceeding joy (Revelation 21:4).

Pray

Dear Lord, thank You that You are my true source of comfort, the One who will wipe away my tears and clothe me in joy. Help me to take the lessons I have learned from You to bring comfort to others in need of Your love. *Amen.*

Apply

① After the resurrection, Jesus appeared to His followers a number of times. Read the account in Luke 24:36–53. What different emotions would the believers have experienced during this encounter?

② Spend some time praising God and thanking Him for all He has done on your behalf.

Acknowledgements

A huge thank you to my editor and publisher, the amazing Anne Hamilton from Armour Books, who believed in this project from the start and gave me the opportunity to share these thoughts with the world. I am so grateful for your suggestions and advice regarding the manuscript and for all the work you put in to make it the best it could be. I also greatly appreciate your insights on stepping over the threshold and into the calling God has for each of us. This book would not have happened in this shape and at this time without some of the breakthroughs I experienced while reading your material. May God bless you a hundredfold for your ministry and generosity.

Thank you to the fabulous Rebekah Robinson from Beckon Creative for your beautiful cover design and layout. They say you can't judge a book by its cover, but you have certainly designed something that will make people want to pick it up and explore.

To my wonderful husband Tim, thank you for your feedback on an early draft of this manuscript and for being the best sounding board a girl could have. Your support and encouragement for this project meant the world to me.

To my dear friend Sandra Henderson, I can't thank you enough for having the courage to share God's word with me. Your ministry and enduring friendship have helped me to walk into my calling and keep going on this journey of a lifetime. May God bless your words as you have blessed me.

And most of all to the Father of all comfort, who comforts me so that I can pass on His blessings to others. Thank you for your patience with me, for the precious gift of your Son Jesus Christ and the presence of your Holy Spirit. I am forever grateful.

www.ingramcontent.com/pod-product-compliance
Lightning Source LLC
Chambersburg PA
CBHW050416120526
44590CB00015B/1992